200

E
& MORE

M000042009

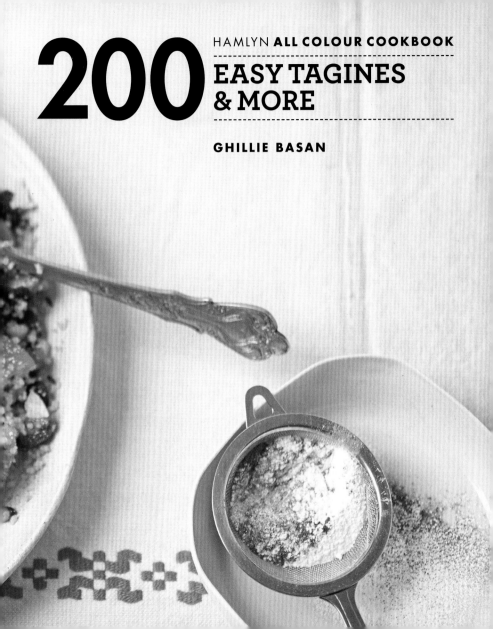

HAMLYN **ALL COLOUR COOKBOOK**

200
EASY TAGINES
& MORE

GHILLIE BASAN

An Hachette UK Company
www.hachette.co.uk

First published in Great Britain in 2015 by Hamlyn,
a division of Octopus Publishing Group Ltd
Carmelite House, 50 Victoria Embankment
London EC4Y 0DZ
www.octopusbooks.co.uk

This edition published in 2016

ISBN 978-0-600-63341-9

A CIP catalogue record for this book is available from the
British Library

Printed and bound in China

10 9 8 7 6 5 4 3 2 1

Standard level spoon measurement are used in all recipes.
1 tablespoon = one 15 ml spoon
1 teaspoon = one 5 ml spoon

Both imperial and metric measurements have been given
in all recipes. Use one set of measurements only and not a
mixture of both.

Eggs should be medium unless otherwise stated. The
Department of Health advises that eggs should not be
consumed raw. This book contains dishes made with raw
or lightly cooked eggs. It is prudent for more vulnerable
people such as pregnant and nursing mothers, invalids,
the elderly, babies and young children to avoid uncooked
or lightly cooked dishes made with eggs. Once prepared
these dishes should be kept refrigerated and used promptly.

Ovens should be preheated to the specific temperature
– if using a fan-assisted oven, follow manufacturer's
instructions for adjusting the time and the temperature.

This book includes dishes made with nuts and nut
derivatives. It is advisable for customers with known
allergic reactions to nuts and nut derivatives to check
the labels of pre-prepared ingredients for the possible
inclusion of nut derivatives.

contents

introduction

introduction

Aromatic and syrupy, zesty and spicy or sweet and fragrant, a dish of tender meat or succulent vegetables simmered to perfection in buttery sauces with fruit, herbs, honey and chillies: tagines are in a class of their own. They are fundamental to the colourful and sensual cuisine of the culinary landscape of Morocco, Tunisia and Algeria, the region referred to as the Maghreb.

Perched at the northwest corner of the African continent, Morocco acts as a culinary gateway to the native influences of central and northern Africa, to the ancient and

medieval traditions of the Arab world and to the Andalucian flavours of southern Spain. From the impressive Atlas and Rif mountains to the majestic cities of ancient dynasties, from the southern deserts with their date-palm oases to the extensive coastline fringed with sun-drenched beaches, Morocco is a land where the medieval and the modern are atmospherically intertwined.

The Arabs, who invaded the region between the 7th and 14th centuries, brought spices, nuts and fruits, some of which were employed in the Persian-inspired meat tagines. The Arabs also brought Islam and its dietary restrictions. The Moors who were expelled from Spain introduced olives, olive oil, tomatoes and paprika to Moroccan cuisine, while Jewish refugees fleeing the Spanish Inquisition brought with them valuable preserving techniques, such as how to make

the ubiquitous preserved lemon. The Ottoman Turks also left their mark with sophisticated pastry-making and kebabs, and the Spanish and French who colonized sections of Morocco had a lasting influence on dishes such as soups and sophisticated fish dishes, as well as café culture, wine-making and the language of the region.

what is a tagine?

Originally a Berber dish, the tagine evolved as the waves of invaders, refugees and colonists left their stamp on the region's cuisine. Classic tagines include combinations of lamb with dried prunes or apricots; chicken with preserved lemon and green olives; duck with dates and honey; fish cooked with tomatoes, lime and coriander; and lentils simmered with turmeric and ginger. Traditional Berber tagines are renowned for their pungent flavouring of clarified or aged butter combined with onions and fiery spices, whereas more modern, French-inspired tagines might include olives and wine.

The name 'tagine' refers to both the cooked dish and the cooking vessel. The traditional vessel is shallow and round and made of clay with a unique conical lid. Other versions include a cast iron base with an earthenware lid. Designed to lock in the moisture and flavours, enabling the food to cook gently in a small amount of liquid, the finished tagine should be served hot from its cooking vessel or transferred into a decorative one.

The secret of an authentic tagine is to simmer the ingredients over a low heat, enabling them to remain deliciously moist and tender. For meat tagines this cooking process may last several hours, allowing the juices of the meat to combine with the oil, liquid and honey to form a rich, velvety sauce. Generally, the pulse, vegetable and fish dishes do not require long cooking times, but the overall taste and texture of the dish benefits greatly from having been cooked in an earthenware tagine.

Traditionally, tagines are cooked over individual, portable clay stoves that are frequently stoked with charcoal to maintain

vessels, whether they are glazed or not, tend to form hairline cracks when they are placed over a gas flame. A heat-diffuser does help in some cases but it is also worth tempering the tagine with scalding milk prior to using it.

choosing & tempering a tagine

If you are planning to buy a tagine in Morocco, Algeria or Tunisia, there are several different types and sizes to choose from. Some represent a tribe, a particular village or a region, while others are used purely for serving, not for cooking. Outside North Africa, there is less choice, but if you are going to use your tagine for cooking, you must make sure it is glazed. Some tagines also benefit from being soaked in water for 24 hours or from being tempered and seasoned by placing bay leaves and dried sage in the base along with a roughly chopped onion, some garlic, and a generous dollop of olive oil, then filled with water and very gently heated through –

a constant heat. This charcoal stove diffuses the heat all around the base of the tagine, enabling the liquid to reduce and thicken without drying out. Tagines can also be used in the embers of open fires, and some traditional versions can be baked in wood-burning ovens. More modern methods employ a gas hob and an electric oven.

choosing a tagine

There are a number of different tagines to choose from but few of the earthenware ones indicate their vulnerability when used over a conventional gas hob. Earthenware tagines cannot be used on an electric ring and, in spite of the accompanying instructions about how to treat your tagine, most of the factory-made

this removes the earthenware taste from the base of the tagine and prepares it for prolonged cooking over heat. Another method of tempering involves filling the base with milk, slowly bringing it to scalding point, and leaving it to cool. By preparing your tagine in this way, you are rendering it heatproof for a traditional charcoal stove, but not necessarily for a gas hob – you may still need a heat diffuser for the hob. Alternatively, you can buy one of the robust cast-iron base tagines with an earthenware conical lid – a very practical option for conventional hob and oven cooking.

Tagines vary in size and depth and are not usually designed for large quantities. A large copper pot, the k'dra, is usually employed for bigger numbers and feasts.

COUSCOUS

In Morocco, tagines are traditionally served as a course on their own with flat breads or chunks of crusty bread to mop up the delectable syrupy sauces. Couscous is usually served separately, but there are some classic dishes in which tagines and couscous are combined. In modern households and tourist restaurants, couscous is often served as an accompaniment to a tagine. A dish of couscous can look spectacular, particularly at banquets when it is piled up in a cone-shaped mound and topped with stuffed pigeons, dates and almonds or decorated with strips of colourful vegetables and topped with sweet onions and raisins tinged yellow with saffron. It is often accompanied by little side dishes, such as spicy chickpeas, herby salads and harissa paste.

Couscous is a traditional staple of the whole of the North African region but it is Morocco's national dish. Although referred to as a 'grain', couscous is not technically one; instead it could be more accurately described as Moroccan 'pasta', as it is made with semolina flour and water and then hand-rolled and dried, even though it is prepared and served like rice. Eating couscous in a traditional manner is an experience in itself and requires a little practice. It is a communal dish so, once the mound has been set on the ground or low table, diners literally ram their right hands, palm upwards, into the grains to extract a handful and then, using the thumb and first two fingers, deftly roll the grains to form tight balls that might incorporate some small pieces of meat or vegetables, and flip them into their mouths. It looks easy, but on first attempts the sauce dribbles down your wrist and the granules spill all over the table.

There are many different types of couscous in Morocco, some made with wheat flour, others with barley, maize or millet. In rural areas, the village women still buy sacks of wheat which they take to the local mill to be ground to semolina, and then laboriously prepare couscous every week by sprinkling the semolina flour with water and raking it with their fingers in a circular motion to form tiny balls. The balls are then rubbed by the palm of the hand against the side of the bowl and passed through a sieve to form a uniform size before being spread out to dry. In modern households in the cities, many cooks prefer to avoid this labour-intensive process and buy sacks of ready-prepared couscous, which need to be steamed several times before being eaten. Outside Morocco and the rest of the Maghreb, the most commonly available packets of couscous have been taken one step further, as the granules are already precooked and only require soaking in water to swell, before being fluffed up and aerated with fingers and a little olive or sunflower oil.

A meal without couscous would be unthinkable to the majority of Moroccans. It is of fundamental value to the culture for dietary, religious and symbolic reasons, as Moroccans believe it is a food that brings God's blessing upon those who consume it. It is therefore prepared in every household on holy days and on Fridays, the Islamic day of rest, when it is traditionally distributed to the poor as well. At festive and religious feasts, such as the traditional gatherings to celebrate births and weddings, a mound of couscous is served as the magnificent dish to crown to end the meal. There is a Moroccan saying that 'each granule of couscous represents a good deed', so it is not surprising that thousands of granules are consumed in a day.

basics,
snacks &
salads

preserved lemons

Makes 1 x 450 g–1 litre (¾–1¾ pint) jar, depending on the size of your lemons
Preparation time **20 minutes**

8–10 **organic unwaxed lemons**, washed and dried
about 10 tablespoons **sea salt**
juice of **3–4 lemons**

Slice the ends off each lemon and stand them on one end. Using a small, sharp knife, carefully make 2 vertical cuts three-quarters of the way through each lemon, as if cutting into quarters, but keep the bases intact. Stuff 1 tablespoon of the salt into each lemon, then pack into a large sterilized jar and seal tightly. Store in a cool place for 3–4 days to soften the skins.

Press the lemons down into the jar until tightly packed, then cover with the lemon juice. Seal the jar and store in a cool place for at least 1 month before using. Use within for 3–4 months.

When ready to use, rinse off the salt and pat dry with kitchen paper. Cut the lemon into quarters and, using a small, sharp knife, remove the flesh, seeds and pith. Finely slice or chop the rind and use as required.

For pickled lemons, pack 8–10 small unwaxed lemons into a sterilized jar. Place 600 ml (1 pint) white wine vinegar, 2–3 tablespoons granulated sugar, 1 tablespoon coriander seeds, 2 dried sage sprigs and 2–3 dried red chillies in a small, heavy-based saucepan and bring to the boil, stirring continuously, until the sugar has dissolved, then reduce the heat and simmer for 5 minutes. Pour over the lemons, seal with a vinegar-proof lid and leave to cool. Store in the refrigerator for 2 weeks before using. (The pickled lemons can be stored in the refrigerator for 4–6 weeks.)

green olives with bitter orange

Serves **4**

Preparation time **20 minutes**

Cooking time **2–3 minutes**

2 teaspoons **coriander seeds**

1 **fresh** or **preserved bitter orange**

450 g (14½ oz) fleshy **green olives**, pitted and finely sliced

2 tablespoons **olive oil**

juice of 1 **lemon**

Dry-fry the coriander seeds in a small, heavy-based frying pan over a medium heat for 2–3 minutes until they give off a nutty aroma, then crush them in a mortar with a pestle to release the flavour.

Peel the bitter orange, remove the pith, and finely slice the rind, discarding the rest.

Place the sliced olives in a bowl. Add the sliced orange rind, crushed coriander seeds, olive oil and lemon juice and mix well. Leave to stand for at least 10 minutes to allow the flavours to mingle. Serve as a starter with bread, if liked, or as a side dish to accompany a tagine.

For cracked green olives with cardamom & harissa, put 350 g (11½ oz) rinsed and drained cracked green olives in a bowl. Dry-roast 1–2 teaspoons cardamom seeds and ½ teaspoon black peppercorns in a small, heavy-based frying pan over a medium heat for 1–2 minutes until they emit a nutty aroma, then crush them in a mortar with a pestle. Add the crushed spices to the olives with 2–3 tablespoons olive oil, the juice of 1 orange and 1 teaspoon harissa paste and mix well.

smen

Makes about **225g (8oz)**
Preparation time **40 minutes**
Cooking time **6 minutes**

450 g (14½ oz) **unsalted
    butter**, at room temperature
100 ml (3½ fl oz) **water**
1 tablespoon **sea salt**
1 tablespoon **dried oregano**

Place the butter in a heatproof bowl and soften by beating with a wooden spoon.

Put the measurement water, salt and oregano in a saucepan, bring to the boil and cook for 4–6 minutes until it has reduced a little, then pour it over the butter and stir with a wooden spoon until well blended. Leave to cool.

Knead the cooled butter with your hands, squeezing out any excess water. Drain well, then spoon the butter into a hot, sterilized jar. Seal the jar and store in the refrigerator, or a cool place, for at least 6 weeks before using. Use within 3–4 weeks.

For clarified butter (ghee), melt 450 g (14½ oz) unsalted butter in a saucepan over a low heat and simmer it very gently for about 45 minutes, making sure it doesn't brown. Strain the clarified butter through a muslin cloth and store in a sterilized jar in the refrigerator, or in a cool place, for at least 6 weeks before using.

dried chilli harissa paste

Makes about **4 tablespoons**
Preparation time **40 minutes,**
   plus 2 days soaking
Cooking time **2–3 minutes**

2 teaspoons **cumin seeds**
2 teaspoons **coriander seeds**
8–10 **dried red chillies,**
   soaked in water for 2 days
3–4 **garlic cloves**, chopped
1–2 teaspoons **sea salt**
4 tablespoons **olive oil**

Dry-fry the cumin and coriander seeds in a small, heavy-based frying pan over a medium heat for 2–3 minutes until they emit a nutty aroma, then grind them to a powder in a mortar with a pestle.

Drain the chillies, chop off the stalks, and squeeze out most of the seeds. Discard the stalks and seeds and coarsely chop the chillies. Using a mortar and pestle, pound the chillies with the garlic and salt to form a thick, smooth paste.

Add the ground spices to the paste and pound again, then beat in most of the oil.

Spoon the paste into a sterilized jar and pour over the remaining oil. Seal the jar and store in a cool place or in the refrigerator. Use within 2 months.

For pickled red chillies, pour 400 ml (14 fl oz) white wine or cider vinegar into a saucepan with 2 tablespoons sugar, 2 teaspoons sea salt and 2 teaspoons coriander seeds. Bring the vinegar to the boil, stirring until the sugar has dissolved, then turn off the heat. Using a small sharp knife, slit 8 red guajillo or serrano chillies down one side, from the stalk to the tip, making sure you don't cut right through them. Pack the chillies in a sterilized jar and pour the vinegar mixture over the chillies to cover completely. Seal the jar and store in the refrigerator for at least 2 weeks before using. Store in a cool place and use within 4–6 months. Serve whole as a starter or slice finely and scatter over salads, tagines or couscous.

herby tomato & caper salad

Serves **4**
Preparation time **20 minutes**

4 large **tomatoes**
finely sliced rind of
  1 **preserved lemon**
  (see page 16)
1 **red onion**, sliced into bite-
  sized pieces
1–2 tablespoons **baby
  capers**, rinsed and drained
small bunch of **flat leaf
  parsley**, finely chopped
small bunch of **coriander**,
  finely chopped
small bunch of **mint**, finely
  chopped
2 tablespoons **olive** or
  argan oil
juice of ½ **lemon**
1 scant teaspoon **paprika**
salt and **pepper**

Place the tomatoes in a heatproof bowl and pour over boiling water to cover. Leave for 1–2 minutes, then drain, cut a cross at the stem end of each tomato and peel off the skins. Cut into quarters, remove and discard the seeds and cut the flesh into thick strips. Place in a large, shallow bowl and add the preserved lemon rind.

Add the onion, capers and herbs to the bowl. Gently toss with the oil and lemon juice and season. Sprinkle over the paprika and serve with warm crusty bread, if liked.

For spicy tomato & preserved lemon salad, thinly slice 4–6 ripe tomatoes and place in a shallow bowl. Add 2 deseeded and finely sliced large green chillies and the finely sliced rind of ½ preserved lemon (see page 16). Drizzle over a little olive or argan oil and season with salt. Gently stir in a finely chopped small bunch of coriander and serve.

chilli & coriander dried fruit & nuts

Serves **4**
Preparation time **12 minutes**
Cooking time **6–8 minutes**

125 g (4 oz) **whole almonds**
2 tablespoons **ghee** or **smen**
  (see page 20)
2 tablespoons **macadamia**
  nuts, halved
2 tablespoons **cashew nuts,**
  halved
125 g (4 oz) **ready-to-eat**
  dried apricots
125 g (4 oz) **ready-to-eat**
  pitted dates
1–2 teaspoons finely chopped
  dried red chilli
grated rind of **1 lime**
small bunch of **coriander,**
  finely chopped
salt

Put the almonds in a bowl and pour over enough boiling water to cover. Leave for 5 minutes, then drain, refresh under cold running water and drain again. Using your fingers, rub the skins off the almonds, then cut the nuts in half.

Heat the ghee or smen in a large, heavy-based frying pan over a medium heat, add the nuts and dried fruit and cook, stirring, for 4–5 minutes until the nuts begin to colour. Toss in the chilli and lime rind and cook for a further 2–3 minutes, then season with salt and stir in the coriander. Serve immediately.

For chilli & coriander mixed nuts, heat 2 tablespoons chilli oil in a heavy-based pan over a medium heat, add 250–350 g (8–11½ oz) mixed nuts, such as almonds, cashews, macadamia and hazelnuts, and cook until they begin to colour. Season with salt to taste and toss in 1 tablespoon finely chopped coriander. Tip into a bowl and serve.

parsnip & beetroot crisps

Serves **4**
Preparation time **10 minutes**
Cooking time about
  20 minutes

sunflower or **vegetable oil**,
  for deep-frying
2 **parsnips**, peeled, halved
  and thinly sliced lengthways
2–3 **beetroot**, peeled and
  thinly sliced
salt and **pepper**

Dukkah spice mix
1 tablespoon **hazelnuts**
1 tablespoon **sesame seeds**
2 teaspoons **cumin seeds**
2 teaspoons **coriander seeds**
2 teaspoons **dried mint**

Make the spice mix. Dry-fry the hazelnuts and seeds in a small, heavy-based frying pan over a medium heat for 2–3 minutes until they emit a nutty aroma. Using a pestle and mortar, pound the nuts and seeds to a coarse powder, or tip into a spice grinder and grind to a fine powder. Stir in the mint and season well. Set aside.

Pour enough oil for deep-frying into a deep saucepan and heat to 180–190°C (350–375°F), or until a cube of bread browns in 30 seconds. Deep-fry the parsnips in batches until lightly golden. Remove with a slotted spoon and drain on kitchen paper, then tip all the parsnips into a bowl while hot, and sprinkle over half the dukkah spice mix.

Reduce the heat (the beetroot slices burn easily) and deep-fry the beetroot in batches. Remove and drain as above, then tip into a bowl and sprinkle with the remaining spice mix. Serve the parsnip and beetroot crisps separately, or mixed together.

For fried bread & dukkah bites, remove the crusts of 4–8 slices of stale bread and cut them into bite-sized squares. Heat enough oil for deep-frying as above. Deep-fry the bread in batches until golden brown. Remove with a slotted spoon and drain on kitchen paper, then tip into a bowl while hot and toss with 1–2 tablespoons ready-made dukkah spice mix (for homemade, see above). Add salt or dried mint to taste and serve.

carrots with cumin & herbs

Serves **4**

Preparation time **5 minutes**

Cooking time **10–12 minutes**

1–2 teaspoons **cumin seeds**

500 g (1 lb) **carrots**, peeled
and cut into thick, bite-sized
sticks

2 tablespoons **olive oil**

juice of 1 **lemon**

2 **garlic cloves**, crushed

1-2 teaspoons **runny honey**

small bunch of **coriander**,
finely chopped

small bunch of **mint**, finely
chopped

sea salt and **black pepper**

Dry-fry the cumin seeds in a small, heavy-based frying
pan over a medium heat for about 1–2 minutes, shaking
constantly, until they emit a nutty aroma. Transfer to a
bowl and leave to cool.

Cook the carrots in a steamer for 10 –12 minutes until
tender. Refresh under cold running water, then drain.

Place the carrots in a bowl and toss with the olive oil,
lemon juice, garlic, roasted cumin seeds and honey.
Season to taste, then stir in the coriander and mint.
Serve as a side dish to accompany tagines.

For carrot salad with orange blossom water & cumin, peel and grate 500 g (1 lb) carrots and transfer to a bowl. Mix together the juice of 1 lemon with 2 tablespoons orange blossom water, half a teaspoon ground cumin and 1 teaspoon honey. Pour the dressing over the carrots, toss to mix well and season with salt and pepper. Serve the salad with tagines.

pink grapefruit & fennel salad

Serves **4**
Preparation time **30 minutes**

1 **fennel bulb**
1 tablespoon **olive oil**
juice of ½ **lemon**
1 scant teaspoon **cumin seeds**, crushed
2 **pink grapefruit**
1 scant teaspoon **salt**
2–3 **spring onions**, finely sliced
1 tablespoon **black olives**, pitted

Cut the base off the fennel and remove the outer layers. Cut in half lengthways and in half horizontally, then finely slice with the grain. Place in a bowl and toss with the oil, lemon juice and cumin seeds. Leave to marinate for 20 minutes.

Meanwhile, using a sharp knife, remove the peel and pith from the grapefruit. Holding the grapefruit over a bowl to catch the juice, cut down between the membranes and remove the segments. Cut each segment in half, place in the bowl and sprinkle with the salt. Leave to stand for 5 minutes to draw out the sweet juices.

Add the fennel to the grapefruit and mix in the spring onions. Serve topped with the olives.

For orange, fennel & apple salad, prepare 2 fennel bulbs as above. Place in a bowl and toss with the juice of 1 lemon. Add 2 cored and finely sliced crispy red or green apples and toss to coat well in the lemon juice. Using a sharp knife, remove the peel and pith from 1 orange. Holding the orange over the salad bowl to catch the juice, cut down between the membranes and remove the segments, then add to the bowl. Dry-fry 1–2 tablespoons shelled pistachio nuts in a small, heavy-based frying pan over a medium heat for 1–2 minutes until they begin to colour and emit a nutty aroma. Using a pestle and mortar, pound the pistachios, 1 garlic clove and a small handful of mint leaves to a coarse paste. Mix with 1–2 tablespoons olive oil, then drizzle over the salad. Season and toss well.

broad beans with mint & lemon

Serves **4**
Preparation time **15 minutes**
Cooking time **4–5 minutes**

750 g (1½ lb) **fresh** or **frozen
    broad beans**, podded
2 tablespoons **olive oil**
juice of 1 **lemon**
finely chopped rind of
    1 **preserved lemon**
    (see page 16)
bunch of **mint**, finely shredded
sea salt and **black pepper**

Fill a large saucepan with water and bring it to the boil. Add the broad beans, return to the boil and cook for 3–4 minutes until tender. Drain the beans, refresh under cold running water and transfer to a bowl.

Add the olive oil, lemon juice, most of the preserved lemon rind and mint to the bowl with the broad beans. Toss well and season with salt and pepper. Garnish with the remaining preserved lemon rind and mint. Serve as a side salad to accompany tagines.

For broad bean dip with preserved lemon, bring a large saucepan of water to the boil, add 750 g (1½ lb) podded fresh broad beans, return to the boil and cook for 3–4 minutes until tender. Drain the beans and refresh under cold running water, then remove the larger beans from their tough skins (the smaller beans don't need to be skinned). Using a mortar and pestle, pound the broad beans with 2–3 peeled garlic cloves to form a smooth paste. Stir in 1 teaspoon ground cumin and 1 teaspoon ground coriander. Gradually beat in 2–3 tablespoons olive oil and the juice of half a lemon. Season to taste with salt and pepper. Spoon the dip into a serving bowl, drizzle a little extra olive oil over the top and garnish with the finely chopped rind of ½ preserved lemon. Serve with toasted flat breads.

orange, date & chilli salad

Serves **4**
Preparation time **30 minutes**

3–4 ripe **sweet oranges**
150 g (5 oz) ready-to-eat soft
    pitted **dates**, finely sliced
2–3 tablespoons **orange
    blossom water**
1 **red chilli**, deseeded and
    finely sliced
finely sliced rind of
    ½ **preserved lemon**
    (see page 16)

Remove the peel and pith from the oranges with
a sharp knife. Place the oranges on a plate to catch
the juice and thinly slice into circles or half moons,
removing any seeds. Place the oranges and juice in
a shallow bowl.

Scatter over the dates, then pour over the orange
blossom water. Cover and leave to stand for 15 minutes
to let the flavours mingle and the dates soften.

Sprinkle over the chilli and preserved lemon rind and
gently toss together.

For orange, radish & chilli salad, using a sharp knife,
remove the peel and pith from 2–3 oranges. Holding
the oranges over a bowl to catch the juice, cut down
between the membranes and remove the segments.
Cut each segment in half, remove any seeds and
place in the bowl. Dry-fry 2 teaspoons fennel seeds in
a small, heavy-based frying pan over a medium heat
for 2–3 minutes until they emit a nutty aroma, then
scatter over the oranges. Add 6–8 sliced small red
radishes, 1 tablespoon pitted and sliced green olives
and 2 deseeded and sliced green chillies. Mix together
2 tablespoons olive oil, 1 tablespoon orange blossom
water and 1 teaspoon runny honey and pour over the
salad. Season, toss together lightly and serve scattered
with 1 tablespoon finely chopped parsley.

couscous

quick cinnamon couscous

Serves **4**

Preparation time **6 minutes**

Cooking time about **4 minutes**

350 g (11½ oz) **couscous**

2 tablespoons **butter** or **ghee**

1 teaspoon **ground cinnamon**

1 teaspoon **icing sugar**
   (optional)

salt and **pepper**

Tip the couscous into a heatproof bowl and just cover with boiling water. Cover with clingfilm and leave to stand for 5 minutes, then fluff up with a fork.

Melt the butter or ghee in a large frying pan over a medium heat, add the couscous, stirring well to separate the grains, and season with salt and pepper.

Spoon the couscous into a pyramid on a serving dish and dust with the cinnamon and icing sugar, if using. Serve hot as a side dish.

For buttered almond & cinnamon couscous, tip 350 g (11½ oz) couscous into a bowl. Stir ½ teaspoon salt into 400 ml (14 fl oz) warm water, pour over the couscous and mix well. Cover with a clean tea towel and leave to stand for about 10 minutes. Melt 2 tablespoons butter or ghee in a heavy-based frying pan over a medium heat, stir in 2 tablespoons flaked almonds and cook for 2–3 minutes until golden brown. Add the couscous and toss well. Serve hot as a side dish, dusted with a little ground cinnamon.

couscous with fennel & courgette

Serves **4**

Preparation time **15 minutes**

Cooking time 10–15 minutes

2 tablespoons **olive oil**

1–2 teaspoons **aniseed seeds**

grated rind of 1 **orange**

2 **fennel bulbs**, trimmed and cut into quarters

juice of 2 **oranges**

1 **courgette**, halved and sliced lengthways

15 g (½ oz) **butter**

1 tablespoon **runny honey**

1 tablespoon **orange blossom water**

salt and **pepper**

½ **orange**, thinly sliced, to garnish

Couscous

350 g (11½ oz) **couscous**

½ teaspoon **salt**

400 ml (14 fl oz) **warm water**

2 tablespoons **olive oil**

15 g (½ oz) **butter**, cut into small pieces

Tip the couscous into an ovenproof dish. Stir the salt into the measurement water and pour over the couscous. Stir once to make sure all the grains are submerged in the water, then cover with a clean tea towel and leave to stand for about 10 minutes. Using your fingers, rub the oil into the grains until light, airy and any lumps are broken up. Scatter over the butter and cover with a piece of damp greaseproof paper. Place in a preheated oven, 180°C (350°F), Gas Mark 4, for about 10–15 minutes until heated through.

Meanwhile, heat the oil in the base of a tagine or a heavy-based frying pan over a medium heat, stir in the aniseed and orange rind and cook for 1–2 minutes until fragrant. Add the fennel and toss to coat well, then pour in the orange juice. Cover and cook gently for 3–4 minutes.

Add the courgette and butter, season and drizzle over the honey. Re-cover and cook for a further 3–4 minutes until the vegetables are very tender. Remove the lid and bubble up any liquid for 3–4 minutes until slightly caramelized, then pour over the orange blossom water.

Pile the couscous on a shallow serving dish and spoon over the fennel and courgettes. Drizzle over the caramelized juice and garnish with the orange slices.

couscous with seven vegetables

Serves **6**
Preparation time **25 minutes**
Cooking time about **20 minutes**

1.2 litres (2 pints) **vegetable
  or chicken stock**
6 **garlic cloves**, peeled and
  smashed
2–3 **rosemary sprigs**
2 **bay leaves**
6–8 **peppercorns**
2 **onions**, cut into quarters
2 **carrots**, peeled and sliced
  lengthways
1 **sweet potato**, peeled and
  cut into long, thick strips
1 **courgette**, halved, deseeded
  and cut into long, thick strips
2 **celery stalks**, cut into 3 pieces
2 **leeks**, cut into 3–4 pieces
2–3 **tomatoes**, quartered
2 teaspoons **honey**
1–2 teaspoons **harissa paste**
sea salt and **pepper**

Couscous
500 g (1 lb) **couscous**
1 teaspoon **sea salt**
600 ml (1 pint) **warm water**
2 tablespoons **sunflower oil**
25 g (1 oz) **butter**, cut into
  small pieces

Tip the couscous into an ovenproof dish. Stir the
salt into the measurement water and pour over the
couscous. Stir once to make sure all the grains are
submerged in the water, then cover with a clean tea
towel and leave to stand for 10–15 minutes. Rake a
fork through the couscous to loosen the grains. Then,
using your fingers, rub the oil into the grains until light,
airy and any lumps are broken up. Scatter over the
butter and cover with a piece of damp greaseproof
paper. Place in a preheated oven, 180°C (350°F), Gas
Mark 4, for 15–20 minutes.

Meanwhile, bring the stock to the boil in a heavy-
based saucepan. Stir in the garlic, rosemary, bay leaves,
peppercorns and 1 teaspoon salt, then add onions,
carrots and sweet potato, reduce the heat and cook
gently for 4–5 minutes. Add the courgette, celery and
leeks and continue to cook gently for 10 minutes, then
stir in the tomatoes, honey and harissa paste and cook
gently for a further 5 minutes. Season to taste.

Pile the couscous in a mound on a shallow serving
dish. Using a slotted spoon, lift the vegetables out of
the stock and place them around the couscous. Pour
the stock into individual bowls and serve with the
vegetables and couscous.

For couscous with steamed vegetables, prepare
and cook the couscous as above. Steam the vegetables
until tender. Arrange them around the hot couscous.
Combine 2 tablespoons olive oil with the juice of
1 lemon, 1 teaspoon harissa paste and 1 tablespoon
finely chopped coriander and drizzle the dressing over
the couscous and vegetables.

couscous with dried fruit & nuts

Serves **4–6**
Preparation time **15 minutes**
Cooking time about **20 minutes**

500 g (1 lb) **couscous**
600 ml (1 pint) **warm water**
1 teaspoon **salt**
pinch of **saffron threads**
3 tablespoons **sunflower oil**
2 tablespoons **smen** (see page 20) or **ghee**
1–2 teaspoons **cumin seeds**
1–2 teaspoons **coriander seeds**
2 tablespoons **flaked almonds**
2 tablespoons **shelled pistachios**
1 tablespoon **pine nuts**
120 g (4 oz) **ready-to-eat, dried apricots**, roughly chopped
120 g (4 oz) **ready-to-eat prunes**, roughly chopped
2 tablespoons **currants** or **raisins**
2 teaspoons **ground cinnamon**
1 tablespoon **icing sugar**

Tip the couscous into an ovenproof dish. Mix together the measurement water, salt and saffron threads and pour over the couscous, stirring once to make sure the grains are evenly spread. Cover with a clean tea towel and leave to stand for 10–15 minutes. Rake a fork through the couscous to break up the grains. Then, using your fingers, rub the oil into the grains until light, airy and any lumps are broken up.

Heat the smen or ghee in a large, heavy-based frying pan over a medium heat, stir in the cumin and coriander seeds and cook for 1–2 minutes to flavour the smen. Add the nuts and cook for a further 1 minute, then add the dried fruit and toss to combine.

Add the nuts and fruit to the couscous and toss lightly to mix. Cover with a piece of damp greaseproof paper and place in a preheated oven, 180°C (350°F), Gas Mark 4, for 15–20 minutes.

Pile the couscous in a conical mound on a shallow serving dish and sprinkle with the cinnamon and sugar – this is usually done in alternate stripes up and down the mound. Serve on its own or as an accompaniment to grilled and roasted meat and poultry.

For pan-fried couscous with nuts, follow the recipe above for soaking and rubbing the oil into the couscous and for frying the nuts and dried fruit. Add the couscous to the frying pan and stir well, making sure it is thoroughly mixed and heated through. Garnish with a small bunch of finely chopped parsley or coriander.

couscous tfaia

Serves **4**

Preparation time **15 minutes**

Cooking time **15–20 minutes**

2 tablespoons **smen**
(see page 20) or **ghee**

3 **onions**, finely sliced

50 g (2 oz) **fresh root ginger,**
peeled and chopped

4 **cinnamon sticks**

2 tablespoons **sultanas** or
golden raisins

1 teaspoon **saffron threads,**
soaked in 4 tablespoons
warm water

1–2 tablespoons **honey**

sea salt and **black pepper**

small bunch of **coriander**,
finely chopped, to garnish

Couscous

350 g (11½ oz) **couscous**

1 teaspoon **sea salt**

400 ml (14 fl oz) **warm water**

2 tablespoons **sunflower oil**

25 g (1 oz) **butter**, cut into
small pieces

Tip the couscous into an ovenproof dish. Stir the salt into the measurement water and pour over the couscous. Stir once to make sure all the grains are submerged in the water, then cover with a clean tea towel and leave to stand for 10–15 minutes. Rake a fork through the couscous to break up the grains. Then, using your fingers, rub the oil into the grains until light, airy and any lumps are broken up. Scatter over the butter and cover with a damp piece of greaseproof paper. Place in a preheated oven, 180°C (350°F), Gas Mark 4, for about 15–20 minutes until heated through.

Meanwhile, heat the smen or ghee in the base of a tagine or a heavy-based frying pan over a medium heat, stir in the onions, ginger and cinnamon sticks and cook for 3–4 minutes to flavour the smen. Add the sultanas or raisins, saffron water and honey, then cover and cook gently for 10 minutes. Season with salt and pepper.

Pile the couscous in a conical mound on a shallow serving dish and use a spoon to create a hollow in the top. Spoon the tfaia into the hollow and around the base of the couscous and garnish with the coriander. Serve as an accompaniment with tagines or grilled dishes.

For couscous with saffron, tip the couscous into an ovenproof dish. Combine the measurment water with 1 teaspoon salt and a scant teaspoon of saffron threads. Leave the saffron to soak in the water for 2–3 minutes, then stir it into the couscous. Cover with a clean tea towel and leave to stand for 10–15 minutes. Follow the recipe above for rubbing in the oil and heating the couscous and serve with tagines.

couscous with apricot chutney

Serves **4**

Preparation time **15 minutes**

Cooking time **25–30 minutes**

225 g (7½ oz) **dried apricots**, finely chopped

1 **apple**, peeled, cored and finely chopped

1 **onion**, finely chopped

3 **garlic cloves**, finely chopped

25 g (1 oz) **fresh root ginger**, peeled and grated

1 tablespoon **sultanas**

2 **cinnamon sticks**

juice and zest of 1 **lemon**

150 ml (¼ pint) **white wine vinegar**

pinch of **chilli powder**

2 tablespoons **honey**

2–3 tablespoons **orange blossom water**

1 tablespoon **sunflower oil**

225 g (7½ oz) **haloumi cheese**

small bunch of **coriander**, finely chopped, to garnish

Couscous

350 g (11½ oz) **couscous**

1 teaspoon **sea salt**

400 ml (14 fl oz) **warm water**

2 tablespoons **sunflower oil**

25 g (1 oz) **butter**, diced

Tip the couscous into an ovenproof dish. Stir the salt into the measurement water and pour over the couscous. Stir once to make sure all the grains are submerged in the water, then cover with a clean tea towel and leave to stand for about 10 minutes. Rake a fork through the couscous to break up the grains. Then, using your fingers, rub the sunflower oil into the grains until light, airy and any lumps are broken up. Scatter over the butter and cover with a damp piece of greaseproof paper. Place in a preheated oven, 180°C (350°F), Gas Mark 4, for 15–20 minutes until heated through.

Meanwhile, make the chutney. Put the apricots, apple, onion, garlic, ginger and sultanas in the base of a tagine or a large, heavy-based saucepan. Add the cinnamon sticks, lemon juice and zest, vinegar and chilli powder, cover and cook gently over a low heat for 15 minutes. Stir the honey and orange blossom water into the apricot and apple mixture and continue to cook for 10–15 minutes until the mixture is thick and fragrant. Season with salt and pepper.

Meanwhile, heat the sunflower oil in a heavy-based frying pan over a medium heat. Cut the halloumi into thin strips and and fry for 2–3 minutes on each side until golden brown.

Pile the couscous in a conical mound on a shallow serving dish and use a spoon to create a hollow in the top. Spoon the chutney into the hollow, arrange the haloumi around the couscous and garnish with coriander. Serve on its own or as an accompaniment with grilled meat and poultry.

couscous with spring vegetables

Serves **4**

Preparation time **15 minutes**

Cooking time about **15 minutes**

850 ml (1½ pints) **hot vegetable** or **chicken stock**

pinch of **saffron threads**

175 g (6 oz) **fresh broad beans**, podded

2–3 **fresh** or **frozen ready-prepared artichoke bottoms**, cut into quarters

4 **baby courgettes**, sliced thickly

4 **garlic cloves**, finely sliced

150 g (5 oz) **fresh peas**, podded

4–6 **spring onions**, thickly sliced

small bunch of **dill**, finely chopped

salt and **pepper**

For the couscous

450 g (14½ oz) **couscous**

½ teaspoon **salt**

500 ml (17 fl oz) **warm water**

1–2 tablespoons **olive oil**

15 g (½ oz) **butter**, cut into small pieces

Tip the couscous into an ovenproof dish. Stir the salt into the measurement water and pour over the couscous. Stir once to make sure all the grains are submerged in the water, then cover with a clean tea towel and leave to stand for about 10 minutes. Using your fingers, rub the oil into the grains until light, airy and any lumps are broken up. Scatter over the butter and cover with a piece of damp greaseproof paper. Place in a preheated oven, 180°C (350°F), Gas Mark 4, for about 10–15 minutes until heated through.

Meanwhile, bring the stock and saffron to the boil in a heavy-based saucepan. Drop in the broad beans, artichoke bottoms, courgettes and garlic and cook for 2–3 minutes. Add the peas and spring onions, reduce the heat and simmer for 10 minutes until the vegetables are tender. Season and stir in the dill.

Pile the couscous on a shallow serving dish. Using a slotted spoon, remove the vegetables from the broth and arrange over the couscous. Drizzle with a little broth and serve the remaining broth separately in a jug.

For preserved lemon & herb couscous salad, tip 350 g (11½ oz) couscous into a bowl. Stir ½ teaspoon salt into 400 ml (14 fl oz) warm water and pour over the couscous. Cover with a clean tea towel and leave to stand for about 10 minutes. Using your fingertips, rub 1–2 tablespoons olive oil into the grains until light and any lumps are broken up. Add 2–3 finely chopped spring onions, 1 deseeded and finely chopped green chilli, the finely chopped rind of 1 preserved lemon (see page 18) and 2 tablespoons each of finely chopped flat leaf parsley, mint and coriander. Season, toss and serve.

cumin couscous with roasted veg

Serves **4–6**
Preparation time **20 minutes**
Cooking time **40 minutes**

1 **aubergine**, cut into bite-
   sized chunks
2 **small courgettes**, cut into
   bite-size chunks
1 **red pepper** and 1 **yellow
   pepper**, cored, deseeded
   and cut into bite-size chunks
4–6 **garlic cloves**, finely sliced
40 g (1½ oz) **fresh root
   ginger**, peeled and cut into
   thin sticks
100 ml (3½ fl oz) **olive oil**
sea salt and **black pepper**
bunch of **coriander**, coarsely
   chopped, to garnish
1–2 **lemons**, cut into
   segments, to serve

Cumin couscous
500 g (1 lb) **couscous**
600 ml (1 pint) **warm water**
1–2 tablespoons **sunflower
   oil**
2 teaspoons **cumin seeds**
25 g (1 oz) **butter**, cut into
   small pieces

Place all the vegetables in an ovenproof dish with the garlic and ginger. Pour over the oil, season well with salt and pepper and place in a preheated oven, 200°C (400°F), Gas Mark 6, for about 40 minutes until the vegetables are tender and nicely browned.

Meanwhile, tip the couscous into an ovenproof dish. Stir the salt into the measurement water and pour over the couscous. Stir once to make sure all the grains are submerged in the water, then cover with a clean tea towel and leave to stand for 10–15 minutes. Rake a fork through the couscous to break up the grains. Then, using your fingers, rub the oil into the grains until light, airy and any lumps are broken up. Toss in the cumin seeds, scatter over the butter and cover with a piece of damp greaseproof paper. Place in the oven for 15–20 minutes until heated through.

Pile the couscous in a mound on a shallow serving dish and spoon the roasted vegetables and cooking juices over and around the couscous. Garnish with the coriander and serve with lemon wedges to squeeze over it.

For cumin & pickled chilli couscous, soak the couscous following the recipe above. Rub 1–2 tablespoons olive oil into the grains to separate them. Deseed and finely slice 2–3 pickled chillies and add them to the coucous with the cumin seeds. Scatter over the butter, cover with a piece of damp greaseproof paper, and place in a preheated oven, 200°C (400°F), Gas Mark 6, for 15–20 minutes to heat through. Garnish with a small bunch of finely chopped coriander.

couscous with dates & cardamom

Serves **4**
Preparation time **15 minutes**
Cooking time **10 minutes**

350 g (11½ oz) **couscous**
400 ml (14 fl oz) **warm water**
1 tablespoon **sunflower oil**
1–2 tablespoons **smen** (see
    page 20) or **ghee**
1 teaspoon **cardamom seeds**
175 g (6 oz) **ready-to-eat
    dried dates**, finely sliced
1–2 teaspoons **ras el hanout**
bunch of **coriander**, finely
    chopped
sea salt and **black pepper**
thick, set yogurt, to serve

Tip the couscous into a heatproof bowl. Stir half a
teaspoon of salt into the measurement water and pour
over the couscous. Stir once to make sure all the grains
are submerged in the water, then cover with a clean
tea towel and leave to stand for 10–15 minutes. Rake
a fork through the couscous to break up the grains.
Then, using your fingers, rub the oil into the grains
until light, airy and any lumps are broken up.

Melt the smen or ghee in a heavy-based frying pan
over a medium heat, stir in the cardamom seeds
and cook for 1 minute. Add the dates and cook for
1–2 minutes, then stir in the ras el hanout. Add the
couscous and stir well, making sure it is thoroughly
mixed and heated through. Season with salt and
pepper and toss in most of the coriander.

Pile the couscous in a mound on a shallow serving dish,
garnish with the remaining coriander and serve with
dollops of yogurt.

For spicy couscous with sultanas, follow the
recipe above, replacing the cardamom seeds with
1–2 teaspoons cumin seeds and substituting the
dates with 3–4 tablespoons sultanas. Serve the
couscous on its own with dollops of yogurt.

couscous with beef & saffron

Serves **4**
Preparation time **5 minutes**
Cooking time **1½–2 hours**

500 g (1 lb) **lean beef**, cut
   into thin strips
1 **onion**, finely sliced
1 teaspoon **ground coriander**
1 teaspoon **ground cumin**
2–3 **cinnamon sticks**
2 tablespoons **sultanas**
2 tablespoons **honey**
pinch of **saffron threads**,
   soaked in 125 ml (4 fl oz)
   warm water
salt and **black pepper**
small bunch of **flat leaf
   parsley**, finely chopped,
   to garnish

Couscous
350 g (11½ oz) **couscous**
½ teaspoon **sea salt**
400 ml (14 fl oz) **warm water**
1–2 tablespoons **sunflower
   oil**
25 g (1 oz) **butter**, cut into
   small pieces

Place the beef, onion, ground spices and cinnamon sticks in the base of a tagine or a large, heavy-based saucepan. Pour in just enough water to cover the meat and bring it to the boil. Reduce the heat, cover and simmer for 1½ hours.

Meanwhile, tip the couscous into an ovenproof dish. Stir half a teaspoon salt into the measurement water and pour over the couscous. Stir once to make sure all the grains are submerged in the water, then cover with a clean tea towel and leave to stand for 10–15 minutes.

Add the sultanas, honey and saffron water to the tagine or saucepan, re-cover and cook gently for 15–20 minutes. Season with salt and pepper. Rake a fork through the couscous to break up the grains. Then, using your fingers, rub the oil into the grains until light, airy and any lumps are broken up. Scatter the butter over the top and cover with a piece of damp greaseproof paper. Place in a preheated oven, 180°C (350°F), Gas Mark 4, for 15–20 minutes until heated through.

Serve the couscous with the beef tagine and garnish with parsley.

For couscous with beef & ginger, prepare and cook the couscous following the recipe above. Heat 2 tablespoons smen or ghee in a heavy-based frying pan over a medium heat, stir in 2 finely chopped garlic cloves and 1–2 tablespoons peeled and finely chopped fresh root ginger and cook for 2–3 minutes. Stir in 225 g (7½ oz) very finely sliced strips of lean beef and cook for 4–5 minutes, stirring continuously. Toss the beef through the prepared couscous. Season and garnish with a bunch of finely chopped parsley.

lemon couscous & spicy shellfish

Serves **6–8**
Preparation time **10 minutes**
Cooking time **10 minutes**

2–3 tablespoons **olive oil**
750 g (1½ lb) **shop-bought ready-prepared seafood selection**
2 teaspoons **harissa paste**
bunch of **coriander**, finely chopped
salt and **pepper**

Lemon couscous
450 g (14½ oz) **couscous**
2 tablespoons **sunflower oil**
finely chopped rind of
  1 preserved lemon
  (see page 16)
25 g (1 oz) **butter**, cut into small pieces

Tip the couscous into a heatproof bowl and just cover with boiling water. Cover with clingfilm and leave to stand for 5 minutes. Fluff up with a fork, then stir in the oil to separate the grains. Transfer to an ovenproof dish, stir in the preserved lemon rind, season with pepper and scatter over the butter. Cover with a damp piece of greaseproof paper and place in a preheated oven, 180°C (350°F), Gas Mark 4, for 10 minutes until heated through.

Meanwhile, heat the olive oil in a heavy-based frying pan over a medium heat, add the seafood and cook for 3–4 minutes. Add the harissa, season and stir in most of the coriander.

Pile the couscous in a mound on a shallow serving dish. Spoon the seafood over the couscous and serve garnished with the remaining coriander.

couscous with tomato sauce

Serves **4**
Preparation time **15 minutes**
Cooking time **20 minutes**

1 tablespoon **olive oil**
1 **onion**, finely chopped
2–3 **garlic cloves**, finely
  chopped
1–2 teaspoons **harissa paste**
1 x 400 g (13 oz) **can
  chopped tomatoes**
1–2 teaspoons **sugar**
bunch of **mint**, finely chopped
bunch of **coriander**, finely
  chopped
salt and **black pepper**
finely chopped rind of ½
  preserved lemon rind (see
  page 16), to garnish

Couscous
350 g (11½ oz) **couscous**
½ teaspoon **sea salt**
400 ml (14 fl oz) **warm water**
1–2 tablespoons **sunflower
  oil**
25g (1oz) **butter**, cut into
  small pieces

Tip the couscous into an ovenproof dish. Stir the salt into the measurement water and pour over the couscous. Stir once to make sure all the grains are submerged in the water, then cover with a clean tea towel and leave to stand for 10-15 minutes. Rake a fork through the couscous to break up the grains. Then, using your fingers, rub the oil into the grains until light, airy and any lumps are broken up. Scatter over the butter and cover with a piece of damp greaseproof paper. Place in a preheated oven, 180°C (350°F), Gas Mark 4, for 20 minutes until heated through.

Meanwhile, heat the olive oil in the base of a tagine or a large, heavy-based saucepan over a medium heat, stir in the onion and garlic and cook for 2–3 minutes. Stir in the harissa, tomatoes and sugar, then cover and cook over a medium heat for 10–15 minutes. Toss in most of the herbs and season with salt and pepper.

Pile the couscous in a conical mound on a shallow serving dish and use a spoon to create a hollow in the top. Spoon the spicy tomato sauce into the hollow and garnish with the rest of the herbs and the preserved lemon rind. Serve with tagines or grilled meat, poultry or fish.

couscous with lemon, feta & mint

Serves **4**
Preparation time **25 minutes**
Cooking time **15–20 minutes**

350 g (11½ oz) **couscous**
400 ml (14 fl oz) **warm water**
1–2 tablespoons **sunflower oil**
finely chopped rind of
  1 **preserved lemon**
  (see page 16)
200 g (7 oz) **feta cheese**, cut
  into cubes
1–2 teaspoons **dried mint**
sea salt and **black pepper**
small bunch of **mint**, finely
  chopped, to garnish

Tip the couscous into an ovenproof dish. Stir ½ teaspoon salt into the measurement water and pour over the couscous. Stir once to make sure all the grains are submerged in the water, then cover with a clean tea towel and leave to stand for about 10-15 minutes. Rake a fork through the couscous to break up the grains. Then, using your fingers, rub the oil into the grains until light, airy and any lumps are broken up.

Stir the preserved lemon rind, feta and dried mint through the couscous until thoroughly mixed, then season with salt and pepper. Cover with a piece of damp greaseproof paper and place in a preheated oven, 180°C (350°F), Gas Mark 4, for about 15–20 minutes until heated through. Garnish with the fresh mint. Serve with tagines or grilled meat and poultry.

For couscous salad with preserved lemon & feta,
soak and oil the couscous following the recipe above. Toss in the finely chopped preserved lemon rind and feta. Omit the dried mint and add 2 tablespoons cracked green olives, pitted and finely sliced, and finely chopped bunches of flat leaf parsley and mint. Toss in the juice of 1 lemon and season well with salt and pepper. Serve with grilled and roasted meat and poultry.

sweet couscous with pistachios

Serves **4-6**
Preparation time **30 minutes**

175 g (6 oz) **raisins**
300 ml (½ pint) **warm tea**
  (made with green or black
  leaves)
450 g (1 lb) **couscous**
600 ml (1 pint) **warm water**
½ teaspoon **salt**
1–2 tablespoons **sunflower
  oil**
1–2 tablespoons **cane sugar**
2-3 tablespoons **orange
  blossom water**
1 tablespoon **ground
  cinnamon**
25 g (1 oz) **butter**
2 tablespoons shelled,
  unsalted pistachios
2 tablespoons **icing sugar**
4 tablespoons **runny honey**
4–6 tablespoons **single or
  double cream**

Put the raisins in a bowl and pour in the warm tea. Leave the raisins to soak for about 1 hour, until nice and plump then drain them thoroughly.

Tip the couscous into a bowl, Stir the salt into the water and pour it over the couscous. Leave it to soak for 10-15 minutes.

Rub the oil into the grains, using your fingertips, and toss in the cane sugar, orange blossom water and half the cinnamon, Add the soaked raisins and mix thoroughly.

Spoon the mixture into a smaller bowl, pressing it down so that it all fits in snuggly, then invert the bowl onto a serving plate, so that you have a couscous dome.

Melt the butter in a skillet and stir in the pistachios for 1-2 minutes, until they emit a nutty aroma. Scatter the pistachios over and around the couscous dome.

Dust the rest of the cinnamon in decorative lines from the top of the dome to the base, and sift the icing sugar over the top.

Heat the honey in a pan and serve the couscous with a drizzle of cream and warm honey as a sweet snack or at the end of a meal.

For couscous with raisins and honey, follow the recipe for the soaking and oiling of the couscous. Toss in 2-3 tablespoons raisins, soaked in tea, and tip the mixture into individual serving bowls. Heat 4-6 tablespoons honey in a small pan and drizzle it over the couscous in each bowl. Serve on its own with yogurt as a quick snack or for breakfast.

beef & lamb

ginger & honey lamb tagine

Serves **4**

Preparation time **5 minutes**

Cooking time **25–30 minutes**

1–2 tablespoons **olive**
  or **argan oil**

1 **onion**, finely chopped

2–3 **garlic cloves**, finely
  chopped

25 g (1 oz) **fresh root ginger**,
  peeled and finely chopped

450 g (14½ oz) **lean lamb**,
  cut into bite-sized pieces

2 teaspoons **ground
  cinnamon**

175 g (6 oz) **ready-to-eat
  dried apricots**

2 tablespoons **runny honey**

salt and **pepper**

Heat the oil in the base of a tagine or a large, heavy-based saucepan over a medium heat, stir in the onion, garlic and ginger and cook for 1–2 minutes to let the flavours mingle. Add the lamb and cinnamon and stir to coat well.

Pour in enough hot water to just cover the meat and bring to the boil. Reduce the heat, cover and simmer for 15 minutes. Add the apricots and honey, re-cover and simmer for a further 10 minutes. Season to taste and serve hot with plain, buttery couscous, if liked.

For spicy ginger & honey lamb tagine, heat 1–2 tablespoons olive oil in the base of a tagine or a large, heavy-based saucepan over a medium heat, stir in 1 chopped onion, 2 chopped garlic cloves, 1–2 deseeded and finely chopped red chillies and 25 g (1 oz) fresh root ginger, peeled and chopped, and cook for 1–2 minutes they begin to colour. Stir in 500 g (1 lb) cubed lamb and 2 tablespoons runny honey and pour over enough hot water to cover. Bring to the boil, then reduce the heat, cover and simmer for 15 minutes. Season to taste and toss in 1 tablespoon finely chopped coriander. Serve with plain buttery couscous or a herb couscous.

spicy meatballs

Serves **4–6**

Preparation time **30 minutes**

Cooking time **about 1¼ hours**

1 tablespoon **olive oil**

1 tablespoon **butter**

1 **onion**, finely chopped

2–3 **garlic cloves**, finely chopped

40 g (1½ oz) **fresh root ginger**, peeled and finely chopped

1 **red chilli**, deseeded and finely chopped

2 teaspoons **ground turmeric**

300 ml (10 fl oz) **water**

small bunch of **coriander**, finely chopped

1 **lemon**, cut into 4–6 segments

Meatballs

450 g (14¼ oz) **finely minced lamb**

1 **onion**, finely chopped or grated

small bunch of **flat leaf parsley**, finely chopped

1–2 teaspoons **ground cinnamon**

1–2 teaspoon **ras el hanout**

sea salt and **black pepper**

Prepare the meatballs. Mix together all the ingredients in a bowl and season. Knead the mixture well, then roll cherry-sized pieces into firm balls.

Heat the oil and butter together in the base of a tagine or large, heavy-based saucepan over a medium heat, stir in the onion, garlic, ginger and chilli and cook for 2–3 minutes to let the flavours mingle.

Add the turmeric and pour in the measurement water. Bring to the boil, then drop the meatballs carefully into the liquid. Reduce the heat, cover and cook gently for 25–30 minutes.

Stir in half the coriander, season with salt and pepper and place the lemon segments among the meatballs. Re-cover and continue to cook gently for about 40 minutes. Garnish with the rest of the coriander and serve with plain couscous, if liked.

For spicy meatballs in a tomato sauce, prepare the meatballs as above. Heat the oil and butter in the base of a tagine or large, heavy-based saucepan over a medium heat, stir in the onion, garlic, ginger, and chillies and cook for 2–3 minutes to let the flavours mingle. Pour in the measurement water. Bring to the boil, then carefully drop the meatballs into the liquid. Reduce the heat, cover and cook gently for about 40 minutes. Stir in 1–2 tablespoons tomato paste, 1 teaspoon sugar and half the coriander. Re-cover and cook gently for a further 20 minutes. Season to taste, garnish with the remaining coriander and serve with couscous.

beef with beetroot & orange

Serves **4–6**

Preparation time **20 minutes**

Cooking time **about 1½–2 hours**

1–2 tablespoons **smen** (see page 20) or **ghee**

3–4 **garlic cloves**, finely chopped

1 **onion**, finely chopped

25 g (1 oz) **fresh root ginger**, peeled and finely chopped

1 **red chilli**, deseeded and finely chopped

2 teaspoons **coriander seeds**

2 **cinnamon sticks**

3–4 **beetroot**, peeled and quartered

500 g (1 lb) **lean beef**, cut into bite-size chunks

1 **orange**, cut into thin segments with the skin on

1 tablespoon **honey**

1 tablespoon **orange flower water**

sea salt and **black pepper**

small bunch of **flat leaf parsley**, finely chopped, to garnish

Melt the smen or ghee in the base of a tagine or a large, heavy-based saucepan over a medium heat, stir in the garlic, onion, ginger and chilli and cook for 2–3 minutes until just beginning to colour. Stir in the coriander seeds, cinnamon sticks and beetroot and cook for a further 2–3 minutes.

Stir in the beef and pour in enough water to almost cover the meat and beetroot. Bring to the boil, then reduce the heat, cover and simmer for 1–1½ hours until the meat is very tender.

Add the orange segments, honey and orange flower water and season with salt and pepper. Re-cover and simmer for a further 15 minutes. Season to taste and garnish with the flat leaf parsley. Serve hot with couscous or fresh crusty bread, if liked.

For beef with orange & ginger, melt the smen or ghee in the base of a tagine or a large, heavy-based saucepan over a medium heat, add the garlic and onion with 50 g (2 oz) fresh root ginger, peeled and finely chopped, and 1–2 teaspoons finely chopped dried red chilli and sauté for 2–3 minutes to let the flavours mingle. Omit the coriander seeds, cinnamon sticks and beetroot, toss in the beef chunks and continue to cook as above.

ginger beef with sweet potatoes

Serves **4–6**
Preparation time **15 minutes**
Cooking time **about 1¼ hours**

2 tablespoons **smen**
(see page 20) or **ghee**
40 g (1½ oz) **fresh root**
ginger, peeled and finely
chopped
1 **onion**, finely chopped
500 g (1 lb) **lean beef**,
cut into bite-size chunks
1–2 teaspoons **ras el hanout**
2 small **sweet potatoes**,
peeled and cubed
600 ml (1 pint) **beef stock**
or **water**
sea salt and **black pepper**
small bunch of **coriander**,
finely chopped, to garnish

Heat the smen or ghee in the base of a tagine or
a large, heavy-based saucepan over a medium heat,
stir in the ginger and onion and cook for 2–3 minutes
to let the flavours mingle. Add the beef, stir to coat
well and cook for a further 1–2 minutes, then stir in
the ras el hanout.

Pour in the stock and bring to the boil, then reduce
the heat, cover and cook gently for about 40 minutes
to cook the meat and flavour the stock.

Add the sweet potatoes and top up the liquid with
water, if necessary, to just cover the beef and sweet
potatoes. Re-cover and cook gently for a further
25–30 minutes until they are tender. Season to taste
and garnish with the coriander. Serve immediately
with plain, buttery couscous, if liked.

For beef with new potatoes, peas & ras el hanout,
follow the recipe above, replacing the sweet potatoes
with 6–8 new potatoes, peeled and cut into bite-size
pieces. After adding the new potatoes to the beef
mixture, cook for 15–20 minutes, then toss in 250 g
(8 oz) peas, re-cover and cook for a further 10 minutes.
Season to taste and garnish with the coriander. Serve
with couscous.

lamb with chestnuts

Serves **4–6**
Preparation time **20 minutes**
Cooking time **about 1 hour 35 minutes**

2 tablespoons **smen** (see page 20) or **ghee**
2 **onions**, finely chopped
3–4 **garlic cloves**, finely chopped
25 g (1 oz) **fresh root ginger**, peeled and finely chopped
1–2 teaspoons **cumin seeds**
1–2 **cinnamon sticks**
500 g (1 lb) **lean lamb**, cut into bite-size pieces
600 ml (1 pint) **lamb** or **chicken stock**
450 g (14½ oz) **shelled chestnuts**
1–2 tablespoons **honey**
seeds of 1 **pomegranate**, with the pith removed

To garnish
small bunch of **mint**, finely chopped
small bunch of **coriander**, finely chopped

Heat the smen or ghee in the base of a tagine or a large, heavy-based saucepan over a medium heat, stir in the onions, garlic, ginger and cumin seeds and cook for 2–3 minutes to let the flavours mingle. Add the cinnamon sticks, stir in the lamb and cook for a further 1–2 minutes.

Pour in the stock and bring to the boil, then reduce the heat, cover and cook gently for about 1 hour to cook the lamb and flavour the stock.

Add the chestnuts and honey, topping up the liquid if necessary to just cover the lamb and chestnuts. Re-cover and cook gently for a further 20–25 minutes until the chestnuts are tender.

Stir in most of the pomegranate seeds, season to taste and cook, covered, for 5 minutes. Garnish with the mint and coriander and the remaining pomegranate seeds. Serve with couscous, if liked.

For lamb with chestnuts & pomegranate syrup,
make as above, replacing the honey with 2 tablespoons pomegranate syrup. Omit the pomegranate seeds and stir some of the chopped mint and coriander into the tagine for the last 5 minutes of the cooking time.

lamb with dates & pistachios

Serves **4–6**

Preparation time **15 minutes**

Cooking time **about 1 hour 25 minutes**

1–2 tablespoons **smen** (see page 20) or **ghee**

2 **onions**, finely chopped

2 **garlic cloves**, finely chopped

700 g (1½ lb) **lean lamb**, cut into bite-size chunks

2 teaspoons **ground turmeric**

2 teaspoons **ground cinnamon**

1 teaspoon **ras el hanout**

250 g (8 oz), **ready-to-eat pitted dates**

1 tablespoon **honey**

1 tablespoon **olive oil**

25 g (1 oz) **butter**

2 tablespoons **shelled pistachios**

sea salt and **black pepper**

small bunch of **flat leaf parsley**, finely chopped, to garnish

Heat the smen or ghee in the base of a tagine or a large, heavy-based saucepan over a medium heat, stir in the onions and garlic and cook for 2–3 minutes to soften them. Add the lamb and stir to coat well, then add the turmeric, cinnamon and ras el hanout.

Pour in enough water to almost cover the meat and bring it to the boil. Reduce the heat, cover and cook gently for 1 hour. Add the dates and stir in the honey, season with sea salt and black pepper then re-cover and cook gently for a further 20 minutes.

Heat the oil with the butter in a small, heavy-based frying pan over a medium heat, toss in the pistachios and cook for 1–2 minutes until they are lightly browned.

Scatter the pistachios over the lamb, garnish with the flat leaf parsley and serve immediately.

For lamb with dates & preserved lemon, follow the recipe above but omit the almonds and pistachios. Finely slice the rind of 1 preserved lemon, adding half of it with the dates and honey and garnishing the tagine with the remaining preserved lemon rind and the parsley.

lamb tfaia with almonds & eggs

Serves **4**

Preparation time **5 minutes**

Cooking time **about 1 hour 25 minutes**

1–2 tablespoons **smen** (see page 20) or **ghee**

2 **garlic cloves**, crushed

1 teaspoon **ground ginger**

1 teaspoon **ground coriander**

1 teaspoon **saffron threads**, ground, using a mortar and pestle, with a pinch of **sea salt**

4–6 **lamb cutlets**

2 **onions**, finely chopped

finely sliced rind of 1 **preserved lemon** (see page 16)

To garnish

4 **eggs**

½ teaspoon **ground saffron**

1 tablespoon **olive oil**

knob of **butter**

2 tablespoons **blanched almonds**

Melt the smen or ghee in the base of a tagine or a large, heavy-based saucepan over a medium heat, stir in the garlic, ginger, coriander and ground saffron. Add the lamb cutlets and sprinkle over the onions. Pour in just enough water to cover the meat, bring to the boil, then reduce the heat, cover and cook gently for 1 hour.

Stir in the preserved lemon rind and season with salt and pepper. Continue to cook gently, covered, for about 20 minutes to let the flavours mingle.

Meanwhile, prepare the garnish. Boil the eggs in a saucepan of boiling water for about 4 minutes so that the yolks are just firm. Drain, allow the eggs to cool slightly, then shell them. Dissolve the ground saffron with 2 tablespoons of warm water in a small bowl and roll the boiled eggs in the yellow liquid to colour them. Cut the eggs in half lengthways and set aside.

Heat the oil and butter in a small frying pan over a medium heat, stir in the almonds and cook for 2–3 minutes until golden brown.

Scatter the almonds over the tagine and arrange the halved eggs around the edge. Serve immediately with crusty bread and a leafy salad, if liked.

For lamb tfaia with olives, follow the method above for cooking the cutlets. Replace the preserved lemon rind with 175 g (6 oz) pitted Kalamata olives and omit the garnish of eggs and almonds. Scatter a small bunch of finely chopped parsley over the tagine and serve with chunks of crusty bread.

meatball & egg tagine with cumin

Serves **4**
Preparation time **10 minutes**
Cooking time **about 25 minutes**

600 ml (1 pint) **water**
15 g (½ oz) **butter**
1 teaspoon **salt**
½ teaspoon **cayenne powder**
4 **eggs**
1–2 teaspoons **cumin seeds**
small bunch of **flat leaf parsley**, finely chopped, to garnish

Meatballs
225 g (7½ oz) **lean minced lamb**
1 **onion**, finely chopped
1–2 teaspoons **dried mint**
1–2 teaspoons **ground cinnamon**
1–2 teaspoons **ras el hanout**
sea salt and **black pepper**

Make the meatballs. Mix together all the ingredients in a bowl and season. Knead the mixture well, then roll cherry-sized pieces into firm balls.

Pour the measurement water into the base of a tagine or a large, heavy-based saucepan and bring to the boil. Add the meatballs, a few at a time, reducing the heat to a gentle boil, and poach the meatballs for 10 minutes, turning occasionally, until cooked through. Remove with a slotted spoon and drain on kitchen paper.

Pour about 125 ml (4 fl oz) of the cooking liquid into the base of a tagine or a large, heavy-based saucepan and bring to the boil. Stir in the butter, salt and cayenne, then add the poached meatballs. Make 4 wells, then break the eggs into the wells, cover and cook for 5–6 minutes, reducing the heat slightly, until the whites are just set but the yolks are still runny.

Meanwhile, dry-fry the cumin seeds in a small, heavy-based frying pan over a medium heat for 1–2 minutes until they emit a nutty aroma. Tip into a spice grinder and grind over the eggs. Garnish with the parsley and serve immediately, with buttered toasted flatbreads, if liked.

For eggs with toasted cumin, heat 1 tablespoon ghee in the base of a tagine or a large, heavy-based, frying pan over a medium heat, break in 6–8 eggs and sprinkle over a little paprika and salt. Cover and cook gently until the whites are firm. Meanwhile, dry-fry 1–2 teaspoons cumin seeds as above. Place in a spice grinder and grind over the eggs. Serve with buttered toasted flatbreads.

baked lamb with quinces

Serves **4–6**
Preparation time **20 minutes**,
  plus marinating
Cooking time **1 hour 45 minutes**

**shoulder of lamb on the
  bone**, about 1.25 kg (2½ lb)
2 tablespoons **olive oil**
1–2 **onions**, cut into wedges
300 ml (½ pint) **water**
40g (1½ oz) **butter**
2 **small quinces**, quartered
  and cored
1–2 tablespoons **honey**
bunch of **flat leaf parsley**,
  finely chopped, to garnish
1 **lemon**, cut into wedges,
  to serve

Marinade
4 **garlic cloves**, chopped
40 g (1½ oz) **fresh root
  ginger**, peeled and chopped
1 **red chilli**, chopped
1 teaspoon **sea salt**
handful of chopped **coriander**
handful of chopped **parsley**
2 teaspoons **ground coriander**
2–3 teaspoons **ground cumin**
3 tablespoons **olive oil**
2 tablespoons **honey**
juice of 1 **lemon**

Prepare the marinade by pounding the garlic, ginger and chilli with the salt in a mortar with a pestle to form a coarse paste. Add the coriander and parsley and continue to pound to a paste. Beat in the cumin, ground coriander, olive oil, honey and lemon juice.

Cut small incisions in the shoulder of lamb with a sharp knife and rub the marinade all over the meat, making sure it goes into the incisions. Cover and marinate in the refrigerator for at least 6 hours or overnight.

Place the shoulder of lamb in the base of a tagine and pour over the olive oil. Scatter the onion wedges around lamb and pour over the measurement water. Cover and place in a preheated oven, 180°C (350°F), Gas Mark 4, for about 1 hour 20 minutes.

Melt the butter in a heavy-based frying pan over a medium heat, add the quinces and stir to coat well, then sauté for 3–4 minutes, depending on size, until golden brown.

Remove the tagine from the oven. Arrange the quinces around the lamb and drizzle the honey over the quinces. Re-cover, return to the oven and cook for 15 minutes, then remove the lid and cook for a further 10 minutes. Scatter the chopped parsley over the top of the lamb and serve with lemon wedges.

spicy beef & sun-dried tomatoes

Serves **4**
Preparation time **8 minutes**
Cooking time **2 minutes**

2 tablespoons **pine nuts**
250 g (8 oz) **ready-cooked
lean beef**, cut into thin strips
150 g (5 oz) **sun-dried
tomatoes in oil**, drained
and cut into strips
2–3 tablespoons **olive
or argan oil**
juice of **1 lemon**
1 teaspoon **harissa paste**
bunch of **flat leaf parsley**,
chopped
salt and **pepper**

Dry-fry the pine nuts in a small, heavy-based frying pan over a medium heat for 2 minutes until golden brown.

Put the beef, tomatoes and most of the toasted pine nuts in a bowl. Mix together the oil, lemon juice, harissa and parsley in a separate bowl and season. Pour over the beef and toss well.

Scatter with the reserved pine nuts and serve with couscous, if liked.

For beef, aubergine & sun-dried tomato tagine,
cut 1 aubergine into bite-sized pieces, place in a colander and sprinkle with salt. Meanwhile, heat 2–3 tablespoons argan oil or ghee in the base of a tagine or a large, heavy-based saucepan over a medium heat, stir in 2 finely chopped onions, 4 finely chopped garlic cloves, 1–2 deseeded and finely chopped red chillies, 25 g (1 oz) fresh root ginger, peeled and finely chopped, and 2 teaspoons coriander seeds and cook for 2–3 minutes to let the flavours mingle. Add 1 tablespoon crumbled dried sage leaves and 450 g (14½ oz) lean beef, cut into bite-sized pieces, and stir well to coat. Pour in 500 ml (17 fl oz) hot beef or chicken stock, bring to the boil, then reduce the heat, cover and simmer for 10 minutes. Rinse the aubergines and pat dry, then stir into the beef, re-cover and cook for a further 10 minutes. Add 125 g (4 oz) sun-dried tomatoes in oil, drained and roughly chopped, and 1 tablespoon runny honey. Season, re-cover and continue to cook for 5 minutes. Scatter over a finely chopped bunch of flat leaf parsley and serve with chunks of crusty bread or couscous.

lamb, sweet potato & okra k'dra

Serves **6–8**
Preparation time **10 minutes**
Cooking time **about
  30 minutes**

2 tablespoons **smen**
  (see page 20) or **ghee**
3 **onions**, finely sliced
2–3 teaspoons **coriander
  seeds**
2–3 **cinnamon sticks**
1 teaspoon **black
  peppercorns**
pinch of **saffron threads**
500 g (1 lb) **lean lamb**,
  cut into bite-sized pieces
1.2 litres (2 pints) **hot lamb**
  or **chicken stock**
2 **sweet potatoes**, peeled
  and cut into bite-sized
  pieces
15 g (½ oz) **butter**
250 g (8 oz) **fresh okra**
juice of **1 lemon**
salt

Heat the smen or ghee in a large copper pot or heavy-based saucepan over a medium heat. Stir in the onions and cook for 1–2 minutes until they begin to soften. Add the coriander seeds, cinnamon sticks, peppercorns, saffron and lamb and mix well.

Pour in the stock and bring to the boil, then reduce the heat, cover and cook gently for 10 minutes. Add the sweet potatoes and butter, re-cover and cook for a further 10 minutes.

Meanwhile, place the okra in a non-metallic bowl, pour over the lemon juice and leave to stand for 10 minutes, then drain.

Add the okra to the pan and simmer for a further 5–8 minutes until cooked through but still retaining a crunch. Season with salt. Serve the lamb and vegetables with couscous, if liked, pouring the sauce into a bowl to serve separately.

For buttered okra with preserved lemon, place 450 g (14½ oz) okra in a non-metallic bowl, pour over the juice of 2 lemons and leave to stand for 3–4 minutes, then drain well. Heat 2 tablespoons olive oil in the base of a tagine or a large, heavy-based frying pan over a medium heat, add the okra and cook for 4–5 minutes until it is tender. Stir in the sliced rind of 1 preserved lemon (see page 16) and season. Pour over 1 tablespoon melted butter and serve with plain, buttery couscous.

beef with prunes & star anise

Serves **4**

Preparation time **10 minutes**, plus soaking

Cooking time **2 hours 30 minutes**

500 g (1 lb) **lean beef**, cut into bite-size cubes

4 **garlic cloves**, smashed in their skins

2 **dried red chillies**

2–3 **star anise**

600 ml (1 pint) **beef stock**

25 g (1 oz) **butter**

1–2 tablespoons **honey**

175 g (6 oz) **ready-to-eat pitted prunes**, soaked in water for 3–4 hours

sea salt and **black pepper**

small bunch of **flat leaf parsley**, finely chopped, to garnish

Place the beef in the base of a tagine or a large, heavy-based saucepan with the garlic, chillies and star anise. Pour in the stock and bring to the boil. Reduce the heat, cover and cook gently for 2 hours.

Season the stock with salt and pepper and stir in the butter and honey. Drain the prunes and add them to the tagine. Re-cover and cook gently for a further 30 minutes to let the flavours mingle. Garnish with the parsley and serve with couscous or chunks of crusty bread, if liked.

For beef with plums & cardamom, replace the star anise with 6 cardamom pods and cook the beef in the stock as above. Season to taste, stir in the butter and honey and cook for a further 15 minutes. Halve and stone 6 firm, fresh plums, add them to the tagine, and cook gently for 10 minutes. Garnish with a small bunch of finely chopped coriander.

lamb chop k'dra

Serves **6-8**
Preparation time **5 minutes**
Cooking time **1 hour
40 minutes**

1 kg (2 lb) **lamb chops**
40 g (1½ oz) **fresh root
ginger**, peeled and finely
chopped
bunch of **flat leaf parsley**,
trimmed and coarsely
chopped
pinch of **saffron threads**
700 g (1½ lb) **Jerusalem
artichokes**, peeled and cut
into bite-size pieces (keep
soaked in cold water with a
teaspoon vinegar until ready
to use)
finely chopped **rind of
1 preserved lemon**
(see page 16)
sea salt and **black pepper**

Place the lamb chops in a large copper pot or heavy-based saucepan and add the ginger, parsley and saffron. Pour in enough water to cover the meat and bring to the boil. Reduce the heat, cover and cook gently for about 1 hour until the meat is cooked and tender.

Drain the artichokes and add them to the pot or saucepan. Top up the cooking liquid if necessary to just cover the meat and artichokes and season with salt and pepper. Re-cover and cook gently for a further 30 minutes until they are tender.

Stir in most of the pickled lemon, season well with salt and pepper and garnish with the remaining pickled lemon. Serve with couscous, if liked.

For lamb with parsley & pickled lemon, heat 1–2 tablespoons smen or ghee in the base of a tagine or a large, heavy-based saucepan over a medium heat, stir in 2 finely chopped garlic cloves and cook for 1 minute. Toss in 500 g (1 lb) lean lamb, cut into bite-size pieces, with a small bunch of finely chopped parsley, the juice of 1 lemon and enough water to cover the meat. Bring the water to the boil, then reduce the heat, cover and cook gently for 1 hour. Season the cooking liquid and stir in the finely chopped rind of 1 pickled lemon. Re-cover and cook gently for a further 20 minutes to let the flavours mingle.

fennel-roasted lamb fillet with figs

Serves **4**

Preparation time **5 minutes**

Cooking time 25 minutes

3 **garlic cloves**, chopped

25 g (1 oz) **fresh root ginger**, peeled and chopped

1 **red chilli**, deseeded and chopped

1 teaspoon **sea salt**

1 teaspoon **ground coriander**

1 teaspoon **ground cumin**

2 tablespoons **smen** (see page 20), **ghee** or softened butter

2 teaspoons **fennel seeds**

700 g (1½ lb) **lean lamb fillet** or **loin**

4 **fresh figs**, halved or quartered

2 tablespoons **runny honey**

salt and **pepper**

small bunch of **coriander**, finely chopped, to garnish

Using a pestle and mortar, pound the garlic, ginger, chilli and salt to form a coarse paste, then add the ground spices. Transfer the paste to a small bowl and beat in the smen, ghee or butter and the fennel seeds.

Cut small incisions in the lamb and rub the mixture all over the meat, pressing it into the incisions. Place the lamb in a roasting tin and roast in a preheated oven, 200°C (400°F), Gas Mark 6, for 15 minutes.

Baste the lamb with the cooking juices, arrange the figs around it and drizzle with honey. Season, then return to the oven and cook for a further 10 minutes until cooked through. Garnish with the chopped coriander and serve thickly sliced, with couscous, if liked.

For roasted fennel & honey figs, cut 8 fresh figs into quarters, keeping the bases intact, and place in an ovenproof dish. Dab a little smen or butter into each one, scatter over 1 teaspoon fennel seeds and drizzle with 1–2 tablespoons runny honey. Place in a preheated oven, 200°C (400°F), Gas Mark 6, for 8 minutes until softened and the honey has melted. Serve with grilled and roasted meats.

chicken, duck, pigeon & rabbit

chicken & green olive tagine

Serves **4**

Preparation time **5 minutes**

Cooking time **about 30 minutes**

1–2 tablespoons **olive** or **argan oil**

2 **garlic cloves**, finely chopped

1 **onion**, finely chopped

1 teaspoon **coriander seeds**

1 teaspoon **cumin seeds**

8 **chicken thighs**

juice of 1 **lemon**

pinch of **saffron threads**

2 **cinnamon sticks**

25 g (1 oz) **butter**

finely sliced rind of 1 **preserved lemon** (see page 16)

175 g (6 oz) **cracked green olives**

salt and **pepper**

Heat the oil in the base of a tagine or a large, heavy-based saucepan over a medium heat, stir in the garlic, onion and coriander and cumin seeds and cook for 1–2 minutes to allow the flavours to mingle. Add the chicken thighs and lightly brown on each side.

Pour in the lemon juice and enough water to just cover the chicken. Stir in the saffron, cinnamon sticks and butter and bring to the boil, then reduce the heat, cover and simmer for 15 minutes. Add the preserved lemon rind and olives, re-cover and simmer for a further 10 minutes. Season to taste and serve hot with the couscous, if liked.

For spicy chicken & preserved lemon pittas, heat 2 tablespoons olive oil and a knob of butter in a frying pan or tagine, stir in 2 crushed garlic cloves and cook for 1 minute, then stir in 1–2 teaspoons harissa paste and 250–350 g (8–11½ oz) ready-cooked chicken, cut into strips and tossed with 2 teaspoons turmeric. Heat through, then add 1 tablespoon chopped preserved lemon rind (see page 16) and 1 tablespoon chopped coriander. Season and spoon into 4 pitta breads. Serve with dollops of natural yogurt and a sprinkling of chopped flat leaf parsley.

spicy chicken with apricots

Serves **4**
Preparation time **5 minutes**
Cooking time **about 1 hour**

2 tablespoons **olive oil**
knob of **butter**
1 **onion**, finely chopped
40 g (1½ oz) **fresh root
  ginger**, peeled and finely
  chopped
1–2 **cinnamon sticks**
8 skinless **chicken thighs**
175 g (6 oz) **ready-to-eat
  dried apricots**
1–2 teaspoons **harissa paste**
2 tablespoons **honey**
1 x 400 g (13 oz) **can
  chopped tomatoes**
salt and **pepper**
small bunch of **coriander**,
  finely chopped, to garnish

Heat the oil with the butter in the base of a tagine or a large, heavy-based saucepan over a medium heat, stir in the onion, ginger and cinnamon sticks and cook for 2–3 minutes to allow the flavours to mingle. Add the chicken thighs and stir to coat well, then cook for 1–2 minutes. Toss in the apricots.

Pour in enough water to cover the base of the tagine or saucepan, bring to the boil, then reduce the heat before covering and cooking gently for 15 minutes.

Beat the harissa, honey and chopped tomatoes together in a bowl, season with salt and pepper and tip the mixture into the tagine or saucepan. Re-cover and cook gently for a further 40 minutes to let the flavours mingle. Scatter the coriander over the top and serve with chunks of crusty bread and a salad, if liked.

For spicy chicken with rosemary & ginger, heat the 2 tablespoons oil with a knob of butter in the base of a tagine or a large, heavy-based saucepan over a medium heat, stir in the 1 finely chopped onion, 40 g (1½ oz) fresh root ginger, peeled and finely chopped and 1 tablespoon finely chopped rosemary and cook for 2–3 minutes to allow the flavours to mingle. Add 8 skinless chicken thighs and stir to coat well, then stir in 1 teaspoon harissa paste and pour in 600 ml (1 pint) water. Bring to the boil, then reduce the heat, cover and cook gently for 1 hour. Season with salt and pepper and serve with couscous.

chicken with artichokes & grapes

Serves **4**

Preparation time **5 minutes,**
  plus marinating

Cooking time **about**
  50 minutes

3 **chicken breasts**, cut into
  bite-size chunks
2 tablespoons **olive oil**
1 **onion**, finely chopped
finely sliced rind of 1
  preserved lemon
  (see page 16)
1 teaspoon **sugar**
1–2 teaspoons **harissa paste**
2 teaspoons **tomato paste**
450 ml (¾ pint) **chicken stock**
  or **water**
1 x 390 g (12½ oz) **can**
  artichoke hearts, drained,
  rinsed and halved
200 g (7 oz) **green grapes**,
  halved lengthways
bunch of **coriander**, finely
  chopped
sea salt and **black pepper**

Marinade
2 **garlic cloves**, crushed
1 teaspoon **ground turmeric**
juice of 1 **lemon**
1 tablespoon **olive oil**

Mix together the ingredients for the marinade in a bowl and toss in the chicken. Cover with clingfilm and marinate in the refrigerator for 2 hours.

Heat the oil in the base of a tagine or a large, heavy-based saucepan over a medium heat, stir in the onion, preserved lemon rind and sugar and cook for 2–3 minutes to let the flavours mingle. Stir in the chicken and cook for a further 1–2 minutes.

Add the harissa and tomato pastes and pour in the stock or water. Bring to the boil, then reduce the heat, cover and cook gently for 30 minutes. Add the artichoke hearts, re-cover and cook for a further 10 minutes.

Stir in the grapes and some of the coriander and cook, uncovered, for 4–5 minutes, then season with salt and pepper. Garnish with the remaining coriander and serve with couscous, if liked.

For chicken with artichokes, olives & capers,
marinate and cook the chicken as above, adding 2 tablespoons pitted green or black olives with the artichokes. Omit the grapes and toss in 2 teaspoons preserved capers for the last 4–5 minutes of the cooking time.

roasted duck legs with quince

Serves **4**
Preparation time **5 minutes**
Cooking time **30 minutes**

4 **duck legs**
3 tablespoons **olive oil**
25 g (1 oz) **butter**
25 g (1 oz) **fresh root ginger**,
    peeled and finely chopped
1 **large quince**, cut into 8
    segments
juice of 1 **lemon**
2 tablespoons **runny honey**
2 teaspoons **ground
    cinnamon**
salt and **pepper**
small bunch of **coriander**,
    finely chopped, to garnish

Rub the duck legs with 2 tablespoons of the oil, season and place in a roasting tin. Place in a preheated oven, 200°C (400°F), Gas Mark 6, for 20 minutes.

Meanwhile, heat the remaining oil and the butter in a heavy-based frying pan over a medium heat, stir in the ginger and cook for 1 minute. Add the quince segments and cook for 2–3 minutes on each side until golden brown. Turn off the heat and pour over the lemon juice.

Pour off any excess fat from the duck legs and arrange the pieces of quince around them. Drizzle the honey over the duck and quince and sprinkle over the cinnamon. Return to the oven and cook for a further 10 minutes until the duck legs are cooked through. Garnish with the coriander and serve with couscous, if liked.

For chargrilled honey & sesame duck skewers, thread 175 g (6 oz) skinless duck breast fillets, cut into thin strips, onto 4 large or 8 small metal skewers. Sprinkle with a little salt and cook over a barbecue or under a preheated grill for 2–3 minutes on each side until just cooked through. Place on a plate and drizzle with 2 tablespoons warmed honey, then roll in a bowl of toasted sesame seeds. Serve at once.

chicken, turnip & chickpea k'dra

Serves **6–8**
Preparation time **5 minutes**
Cooking time **27 minutes**

2–3 tablespoons **smen**
(see page 20) or **ghee**
4 **onions**, finely chopped
2 teaspoons **cumin seeds**
2–3 **cinnamon sticks**
pinch of **saffron threads**
12 **chicken thighs**, skinned
1 x 450 g (14½ oz) **can
chickpeas**, rinsed and
drained
1.2 litres (2 pints) **hot chicken
stock**
450 g (14½ oz) **peeled
turnips**, cut into bite-sized
chunks
2 tablespoons **sultanas**
1 teaspoon **sea salt**
1 teaspoon **black pepper**
½ tablespoon **butter**
bunch of **flat leaf parsley**,
finely chopped

Heat the smen or ghee in a large copper pot or heavy-based saucepan over a medium heat, stir in the onions, cumin seeds, cinnamon sticks and saffron and cook for 1–2 minutes to let the flavours mingle. Add the chicken and stir to coat well, then add the chickpeas.

Pour in the stock and bring to the boil, then reduce the heat, cover and cook over a medium heat for 15 minutes.

Add the turnips and sultanas, re-cover and cook over a medium heat for a further 10 minutes until the chicken is cooked through. Season with the salt and pepper and stir in the butter and parsley. Serve the chicken, chickpeas and turnip with couscous, if liked, pouring the sauce into a bowl to serve separately.

For saffron onions & sultanas, heat 1–2 tablespoons smen or ghee in the base of a tagine or a large, heavy-based saucepan, stir in 3–4 finely sliced or chopped onions and cook for 1–2 minutes to soften. Add 2 tablespoons sultanas and a pinch of saffron threads, cover and cook gently for 8 minutes. Season with a little salt and serve the onion mixture as a side dish with k'dras or couscous.

spicy pigeons with olives

Serves **2**

Preparation time **5 minutes**

Cooking time **about 1 hour 20 minutes**

1 tablespoon **tomato paste**

1 teaspoon **sugar**

1 teaspoon **paprika**

1 teaspoon **ground cinnamon**

1 teaspoon **ground cumin**

1 teaspoon **ground coriander**

1–2 tablespoons **smen** (see page 20) or **ghee**

2 **fresh wood pigeons**, prepared by a butcher, cleaned and left whole

4 **bay leaves**

4 **cloves**

juice of 1 **lemon**

300 ml (½ pint) **water**

8–10 **cracked green olives**

sea salt and **black pepper**

Mix together the tomato paste with the sugar and spices in a small bowl and set aside.

Melt the smen or ghee in the base of a tagine or a large, heavy-based saucepan over a medium heat. Place the pigeons, breast-side down, in the tagine or saucepan and cook for 2–3 minutes until the breasts are lightly brown. Transfer the pigeons to a plate.

Add the spicy tomato paste, bay leaves, cloves, lemon juice and measurement water to the tagine or saucepan and stir to mix well. Return the pigeons to the tagine or saucepan, cover and cook gently for about 1 hour, turning the pigeons in the sauce from time to time until they are tender.

Add the olives and cook gently for a further 15 minutes. Season with salt and pepper and serve hot with chunks of bread to mop up the sauce, if liked.

For spicy quails with olives, brown and cook 2–4 oven-ready quails in the same way as for the pigeons in the recipe above, reducing the cooking time to 40 minutes before adding the olives together with the finely chopped rind of one preserved lemon (see page 16).

duck with cherries & cinnamon

Serves **4**

Preparation time **20 minutes**

Cooking time **1 hour
5 minutes**

1–2 tablespoons **smen**
(see page 20) or **ghee**

1 **onion**, finely chopped

2–3 **garlic cloves**, finely
chopped

2 teaspoons **coriander seeds**

3–4 **cinnamon sticks**

3 **duck breasts**, cut into bite-
size chunks

juice of 1 **lemon**

225 g (7½ oz) **fresh sour
cherries**, pitted

1–2 tablespoons **honey**

sea salt and **black pepper**

To garnish

small bunch of **flat leaf
parsley**

small bunch of **mint**

Melt the smen or ghee in the base of a tagine
or a large, heavy-based saucepan over a medium heat,
stir in the onion, garlic, coriander seeds and cinnamon
sticks and cook for 2–3 minutes to let the flavours
mingle. Add the duck breasts and stir to coat well.

Pour in the lemon juice and just enough water to cover
the duck. Bring to the boil, then reduce the heat before
covering and cook gently for 40 minutes.

Stir in the cherries and honey and cook gently for
a further 20 minutes. Season with salt and pepper,
garnish with the parsley and mint, and serve the tagine
with couscous, if liked.

For pheasant with cranberries & cinnamon,

ask your butcher to prepare 2 pheasant, to give
you 4 breasts. Cook the pheasant in the same way
as the duck in the recipe above, replacing the sour
cherries with 200 g (7 oz) fresh cranberries.
Garnish with a small bunch of finely chopped parsley
or coriander.

chicken with mallow leaves

Serves **4–6**
Preparation time **10 minutes**
Cooking time **about 1 hour 20 minutes**

1 **small chicken**, about 1.25–1.5 kg (2½–3 lb)
1 **onion**, quartered
2 **carrots**, peeled and thickly sliced
4 **garlic cloves**, smashed in their skins
4 **cloves**
4 **cardamom pods**
6 **black peppercorns**
200 g (7 oz) **dried mallow leaves**
sea salt

Place the chicken in the base of a large tagine or heavy-based saucepan and add the onion, carrots, garlic, cloves, cardamom pods and peppercorns. Pour in just enough water to come up the sides of the tagine base to halfway up the chicken and bring to the boil, then reduce the heat, cover and cook gently for 40 minutes, turning the chicken in the stock once or twice during this time.

Meanwhile, use your hands to crush the dried mallow and place them in a heatproof bowl. Pour over just enough boiling water to cover and leave to stand for 30 minutes.

Drain the mallow leaves and add them to the tagine or saucepan. Re-cover and cook gently for a further 30 minutes.

Lift the chicken out of the tagine or saucepan and set on a chopping board. Using a sharp knife, remove the skin and cut the chicken into joints.

Season the cooking liquid and return the chicken joints to the tagine or saucepan. Toss the chicken joints gently in the cooking liquid for 2–3 minutes to heat through. Serve with chunks of bread or couscous, if liked.

For chicken with spinach, cook the chicken with the onion, carrots, garlic and spices for 1 hour as above. Add 250 g (8 oz) fresh spinach leaves to the tagine instead of the mallow leaves and cook for a further 10 minutes so that the spinach wilts. Stir the spinach into the cooking liquid when you remove and joint the chicken, then return the chicken joints to the pan as above. Serve the tagine with chunks of bread.

rabbit with chillies & aubergines

Serves **2–4**

Preparation time **20 minutes**

Cooking time **about 1 hour
10 minutes**

1–2 tablespoons **smen**
(see page 20) or **ghee**

1 **onion**, halved and sliced

2–3 **garlic cloves**, chopped

2 teaspoons finely chopped
dried red chillies

2 teaspoons **coriander seeds**

1 teaspoon **cumin seeds**

1 **rabbit**, about 1.25–1.5 kg
(2½–3 lb), cleaned and
jointed

300 ml (½ pint) **water**

1 x 400 g (13 oz) **can
chopped tomatoes**

1–2 teaspoons **sugar**

small bunch of **coriander**,
finely chopped

1 **aubergine**, diced

sea salt and **black pepper**

Heat the smen or ghee in the base of a large tagine or heavy-based saucepan over a medium heat, stir in the onion, garlic, chillies and coriander and cumin seeds and cook for 2–3 minutes to let the flavours mingle. Add the rabbit joints, stir to coat well and cook for a further 1–2 minutes.

Pour in the measurement water and add the chopped tomatoes, sugar and most of the coriander. Bring to the boil, then reduce the heat, cover and cook gently for 45 minutes.

Add the aubergine, re-cover and cook gently for a further 15–20 minutes until the aubergine is soft and has absorbed the flavours. Season to taste with salt and pepper. Garnish with the remaining coriander and serve with chunks of fresh crusty bread, if liked.

For rabbit with cherry tomatoes, follow the recipe above, tossing the rabbit joints in the onion, garlic, chillies and spices. Pour in enough water to just cover the rabbit, bring to the boil, then reduce the heat, cover and cook gently for 50 minutes. Season, stir in 2 teaspoons honey and toss in 8–10 cherry tomatoes with a bunch of finely chopped coriander. Re-cover and cook gently for 10–15 minutes until the tomatoes are soft. Serve with couscous.

pigeon with prunes & honey

Serves **3–4**
Preparation time **10 minutes**
Cooking time **25–30 minutes**

2 tablespoons **olive oil**
2 **garlic cloves**, finely chopped
25 g (1 oz) **fresh root ginger**,
   peeled and finely chopped
2 **cinnamon sticks**
6–8 **wood pigeon breasts**
pinch of **saffron threads**
175 g (6 oz) **ready-to-eat
   pitted prunes**
300 ml (½ pint) **water**
1 tablespoon **honey**
25 g (1 oz) **butter**
sea salt and **black pepper**
1 teaspoon **icing sugar**,
   for dusting
1 teaspoon **ground
   cinnamon**, for dusting

Heat the oil in the base of a tagine or a large, heavy-based saucepan over a medium heat, stir in the garlic, ginger and cinnamon sticks and cook for 2–3 minutes to let the flavours mingle. Add the pigeon breasts and quickly sear them on all sides, then transfer to a chopping board and cut them into thick strips. Cover and set aside.

Stir the saffron and prunes into the tagine or saucepan and pour in the measurement water. Add the honey and butter. Bring to the boil, then reduce the heat, cover and cook gently for 15–20 minutes. Season to taste with salt and pepper.

Return the pigeon strips to the tagine or saucepan and cook gently for 4–5 minutes to heat through. Dust with icing sugar and cinnamon and serve with chunks of crusty bread, if liked.

For chicken livers with prunes & honey, replace the pigeon breasts with 225 g (7½ oz) trimmed chicken livers. Sear the chicken livers in the oil with the garlic and ginger as above, omitting the cinnamon sticks, then transfer the chicken livers to a plate and set aside. Proceed with the recipe above, returning the chicken livers to the tagine or saucepan for the last 5 minutes of cooking time. Omit the ground cinnamon and icing sugar and garnish with a bunch of finely chopped flat leaf parsley.

duck with raisins & pickled lemons

Serves **4**

Preparation time **15 minutes**

Cooking time **1 hour**

4 **duck legs**

2 teaspoons **ras el hanout**

40 g (1½ oz) **fresh root ginger**, peeled and grated

1 **onion**, grated

pinch **dried sage leaves**, crumbled

juice of 1 **lemon**

2–3 tablespoons **raisins**

finely sliced rind of 1 **pickled lemon** (see page 16)

seeds of ½ **pomegranate**

bunch of **flat leaf parsley**, finely chopped

sea salt and **black pepper**

Rub the duck legs with the ras el hanout and place them in the base of a large tagine or heavy-based saucepan. Add the ginger, onion and dried sage and pour in the lemon juice and enough water to come halfway up the duck. Bring to the boil, then reduce the heat, cover and cook gently for 40 minutes.

Stir in the raisins and the pickled lemon rind, re-cover and cook gently for a further 20 minutes to let the flavours mingle. Season to taste with salt and pepper. Toss in most of the pomegranate seeds and some of the parsley. Garnish with the remaining pomegranate seeds and parsley and serve with couscous, if liked.

For quails with pickled lemons & pomegranate seeds, place 4 oven-ready quails in the base of a tagine or large, heavy-based saucepan and rub them with 2 teaspoons ras el hanout. Scatter over 40 g (1½ oz) fresh root ginger, peeled and grated, and 1 grated onion and pour in the juice of 1 lemon and enough water to just cover the quail. Bring to the boil, then reduce the heat, cover, and cook gently for 30 minutes. Season with salt and pepper, add the finely sliced rind of 1 pickled lemon and most of the seeds from ½ pomegranate and cook, covered, for a further 10 minutes. Garnish with the remaining pomegranate seeds and serve with chunks of crusty bread.

chicken with courgettes & mint

Serves **4**
Preparation time **20 minutes**
Cooking time **about 1 hour**

8 **small shallots**, peeled
8 **garlic cloves**, peeled
3 **chicken breasts**, cut into
   bite-size chunks
1 teaspoon **fennel seeds**
1 teaspoon **cumin seeds**
1 teaspoon **dried mint**
1 tablespoon **olive oil**
3–4 tablespoons **white wine**
   or **cider vinegar**
2 **courgettes**, cut into bite-size
   chunks
sea salt and **black pepper**
bunch of **mint**, finely chopped,
   to garnish

Place the shallots, garlic and chicken breasts in the base of a tagine or a large, heavy-based saucepan and scatter over the fennel and cumin seeds and dried mint. Pour in just enough water to cover the chicken and drizzle in the oil. Bring to the boil, then reduce the heat, cover and cook gently for 40 minutes.

Stir in the vinegar and courgettes and season with salt and pepper. Re-cover and cook gently for a further 15–20 minutes until the courgettes are tender and the flavours have mingled. Garnish with the fresh mint and serve with couscous, if liked.

For chicken with mint and lemon, place 8 skinless chicken thighs in the base of a tagine or large, heavy-based saucepan with 4 sliced shallots and 4 finely chopped garlic cloves. Add 1 teaspoon each of fennel seeds, cumin seeds and dried mint. Combine the juice of 1 lemon with 2 tablespoons olive oil and 100 ml (3½ fl oz) water and pour over the chicken. Bring to the boil, then reduce the heat, cover and cook gently for 30 minutes. Cut 1 lemon into thin segments and tuck them between the chicken thighs. Re-cover and cook gently for a further 30 minutes to let the flavours mingle. Season to taste with salt and pepper. Garnish with the fresh mint and serve with couscous.

rabbit mrouzia

Serves **2**
Preparation time **20 minutes**
Cooking time **1 hour**

1 medium-sized **rabbit**,
   cleaned and cut into joints
2 teaspoons **ras el hanout**
125 g (4 oz) **butter**, cut into
   small pieces
2 **onions**, grated
150 g (5 oz) **blanched
   almonds**
150 g (5 oz) **sultanas**
2 tablespoons **honey**
sea salt and **black pepper**
scant teaspoon **ground
   cinnamon**, for dusting

Place the rabbit in the base of a tagine or a large, heavy-based saucepan. Rub the ras el hanout over the rabbit. Add the butter, grated onions and almonds and pour in enough water to cover the rabbit. Bring to the boil, then reduce the heat, cover and cook gently for 40 minutes.

Using a slotted spoon, remove the rabbit pieces and set aside on a plate. Stir the sultanas and honey into the cooking liquid, season with salt and pepper and cook over a high heat for 10 minutes to reduce and thicken the sauce.

Return the rabbit pieces to the tagine or saucepan, stir to coat well and cook over a medium heat for about 10 minutes until heated through. Dust with the cinnamon and serve with couscous, if liked.

For hare mrouzia, replace the rabbit with 1 cleaned and jointed hare and cook as above, allowing an extra 15–20 minutes cooking time before adding the sultanas and honey, together with a small bunch of finely chopped sage leaves.

baked chicken with saffron

Serves **4–6**
Preparation time **10 minutes**
Cooking time **1 hour**
  15 minutes

pinch of **saffron threads**
100 ml (3½ fl oz) **warm water**
1 **chicken** about 2 kg
  (4 lb 8 oz)
1 teaspoon **sea salt**
2 tablespoons **olive oil**
juice of 1 **lemon**
2 tablespoons **orange**
  blossom water
bunch of **flat leaf parsley**,
  finely chopped
bunch of **dill**, finely chopped
bunch of **mint**, finely chopped
25 g (1 oz) **butter**, cut into
  small pieces

Stir the saffron into the warm water in a small bowl and leave to stand for 5–10 minutes.

Place the chicken in the base of a large tagine. Rub the salt all over the chicken.

Combine the olive oil, lemon juice and orange blossom water in a bowl. Add the saffron water and stir in most of the chopped herbs, then pour the mixture over the chicken.

Cover and place the tagine in a preheated oven, 180°C (350°F), Gas Mark 4, for 1 hour, basting the chicken with the cooking juices from time to time.

Scatter the butter over the chicken, then return to the oven, uncovered, for 15 minutes until the chicken browns lightly on top. Garnish with the remaining parsley, mint, and dill and serve with couscous and a salad, if liked.

For quails baked with herbs and lemon, rub 4 oven-ready quails with salt and place them in the base of a tagine. Combine the olive oil, lemon juice and orange blossom water with the parsley dill and mint as above, adding the finely chopped rind of 1 preserved lemon and 2 tablespoons water to the bowl. Pour the mixture over the quails, cover and place in a preheated oven, 180°C (350°F), Gas Mark 4, for 30 minutes. Scatter the butter over the quails and return to the oven, uncovered, for 10–15 minutes until the quails brown lightly on top. Serve with chunks of bread to mop up the buttery juices.

fish & shellfish

chermoula monkfish & olive tagine

Serves **4**
Preparation time **5 minutes**
Cooking time **10–15 minutes**

700 g (1 ½ lb) **monkfish tail**,
   cut into bite-sized pieces
2 tablespoons **ready-made
   chermoula paste**
2 tablesoons **olive oil**
2 tablespoons **marinated
   black olives**, drained and
   pitted
50 ml (2 fl oz) **fino sherry**
salt and **pepper**

To garnish
smoked paprika
finely chopped **flat leaf
   parsley**

Place the monkfish tail in a bowl, rub with the
chermoula and leave to marinate for 5 minutes.

Heat the oil in the base of a tagine or a large, heavy-
based frying pan over a medium heat, stir in the
monkfish, olives and sherry, cover and cook for 10–15
minutes until the fish is cooked through. Season, then
serve sprinkled with a little paprika and parsley.

For steamed monkfish with chermoula & couscous,
line a steamer with coriander leaves and place 700 g
(1 ½ lb) monkfish tail, cut into bite-sized pieces, on top.
Steam for 8–10 minutes until just cooked through and
tender. Season and serve hot with a bowl of ready-made
chermoula paste for dipping. Serve with a herby or spicy
couscous.

shellfish with fennel & harissa

Serves **4**
Preparation time **15 minutes**
Cooking time **about**
  10 minutes

450 g (14½ oz) **live mussels**
2 tablespoons **olive oil**
3–4 **shallots**, finely chopped
1 **fennel bulb**, trimmed and
  finely sliced
1–2 teaspoon **harissa paste**
300 ml (½ pint) **water**
juice of **1 lemon**
450 g (14½ oz) **raw prawns**
  in their shells, thoroughly
  rinsed
large bunch of **coriander**,
  finely chopped
sea salt and **black pepper**

Scrub the mussels in plenty of cold water. Scrape off any barnacles and beards with a knife and discard any mussels that fail to open when lightly tapped on a work surface. Rinse well, then drain.

Heat the oil in the base of a tagine or a large, heavy-based saucepan over a medium heat, stir in the shallots and fennel and cook for 2–3 minutes until they begin to soften. Stir in the harissa, pour in the measurement water and lemon juice and bring to the boil.

Add the mussels and prawns to the tagine, reduce the heat, cover and cook gently for 5–6 minutes, or until the mussels open. Discard any that remain shut. Season, stir in the coriander and serve with couscous, if liked.

For shellfish with tomato & harissa, add 1 x 400 g (13 oz) can chopped tomatoes to the tagine with the harissa paste. Stir in 1 teaspoon of sugar and 1 tablespoon of the chopped coriander, then pour in the water, omitting the lemon juice, and cook as above.

fish with preserved lemon & mint

Serves **4**

Preparation time **20 minutes**,
  plus marinating

Cooking time about **25
  minutes**

700 g (1½ lb) **fresh fish
  fillets**, such as **cod** or
  haddock, cut into large chunks
2 tablespoons **olive oil**
1 **onion**, finely chopped
2 **celery sticks**, finely chopped
finely chopped rind of
  1 **preserved lemon**
  (see page 16)
300 ml (½ pint) **fish stock** or
  water
150 ml (¼ pint) **white wine** or
  fino sherry
sea salt and **black pepper**
bunch of **mint**, finely chopped

Chermoula
2–3 **garlic cloves**, chopped
1 **red chilli**, deseeded and
  chopped
1 teaspoon **sea salt**
small bunch of **coriander**
pinch of **saffron threads**
1–2 teaspoons **ground cumin**
3–4 tablespoons **olive oil**
juice of 1 **lemon**

Make the chermoula. Place the garlic, chilli and salt
in a mortar and pound with a pestle to form a paste.
Add the coriander leaves and pound to a coarse paste.
Beat in the saffron, cumin, olive oil and lemon juice.

Transfer the chermoula to a large bowl, Add the fish
chunks and stir to coat well. Cover with clingfilm and
leave to marinate in the refrigerator for 1–2 hours.

Heat the oil in the base of a tagine or a large, heavy-
based saucepan over a medium heat, stir in the onion
and celery and cook for 2–3 minutes until they begin
to soften.

Stir in the preserved lemon rind and pour in the stock
or water and wine or sherry. Bring to the boil, then
reduce the heat, cover and simmer for 10–15 minutes.
Season with salt and pepper.

Add the marinated fish and the remaining marinade
to the tagine, re-cover and cook gently for a further
5 minutes until the fish is cooked through. Stir a little
of the mint through the tagine and garnish with the
remaining mint. Serve with plain couscous, if liked.

For prawns & scallops with preserved lemon &
mint, replace the fish fillets with 400 g (13 oz) shelled
scallops and 400 g (13 oz) shelled prawns. Marinate
them in the chermoula for 1 hour, then follow the recipe
above, adding a little extra stock or wine if necessary to
keep the fish and shellfish just covered.

oven-baked red mullet

Serves **2**

Preparation time **15 minutes**

Cooking time **25 minutes**

2 tablespoons **olive oil**

25 g (1 oz) **butter**

2–3 **garlic cloves**, finely sliced

2 x **red mullet**, gutted and
    cleaned, approximately
    250 g (9 oz) in total

sea salt

2 **tomatoes**, finely sliced

1 **lime**, finely sliced

small bunch of **flat leaf
    parsley**, finely chopped,
    to garnish

1 **lemon**, cut into wedges,
    to serve

Heat the olive oil and butter in the base of a tagine
over a medium heat, stir in the garlic and cook for
1–2 minutes until it begins to colour. Place the fish
in the tagine and cook for approximately 2 minutes
on each side until lightly brown.

Remove the tagine from the heat, scatter a little salt
over the fish and arrange the slices of tomato and lime
over the top of the fish.

Cover and place in a preheated oven, 180°C (350°F),
Gas Mark 4, for about 15 minutes. Remove the lid and
bake for a further 5 minutes until the fish is cooked
through. Scatter the parsley over the top and serve with
wedges of lemon to squeeze over the fish.

For baked red mullet with preserved lemon, heat
2 tablespoons olive oil and 25 g (1 oz) butter in the
base of a tagine over a medium heat, stir 2–3 finely
sliced garlic cloves and adding 2 teaspoons coriander
seeds and cook for 1–2 minutes to flavour the oil.
Place the fish in the tagine and cook for approximately
2 minutes on each side until lightly brown. Remove the
tagine from the heat and arrange the finely sliced rind
of 2 preserved lemons over the top of the fish. Cover
and place in a preheated oven, 180°C (350°F), Gas
Mark 4, for about 15 minutes. Remove the lid and bake
for a further 5 minutes until the fish is cooked through.
Scatter 1 small bunch of finely chopped parsley over
the top and serve with wedges of lemon to squeeze
over the fish.

saffron & herb fish tagine

Serves **4**
Preparation time **5 minutes**
Cooking time **15 minutes**

pinch of **saffron threads**
300 ml (½ pint) **warm water**
1–2 tablespoons **olive oil**
finely sliced rind of
   1 **preserved lemon**
   (see page 16)
500 g (1 lb) skinless, firm-
   fleshed **fish fillets**, such as
   sea bass, cut into chunks
small bunch of **mint**, finely
   chopped
salt and **pepper**

Dry-fry the saffron in a small frying pan over a medium heat for less than a minute until it emits a faint aroma. Using a pestle and mortar or spice grinder, grind to a powder, then stir in the measurement water until the saffron dissolves.

Heat the oil in the base of a tagine or a large, heavy-based saucepan. Stir in the preserved lemon rind, fish, most of the mint and the saffron water and season with salt and pepper. Bring to the boil, then reduce the heat, cover and cook gently, stirring occasionally, for 15 minutes until the fish is cooked through. Garnish with the reserved mint and serve with couscous, if liked.

For sea bass with olives, saffron & preserved
lemon, heat 2 tablespoons olive oil in the base of a tagine or a large, heavy-based saucepan over a medium heat, stir in a pinch of saffron threads, 2 tablespoons finely sliced green olives and 1 tablespoon finely sliced preserved lemon rind (see page 16) and cook for 1–2 minutes to let the flavours mingle. Add 500 g (1 lb) skinless, firm-fleshed fish fillets, such as sea bass, cut into bite-sized pieces, and cook for a further 2–3 minutes. Season, cover and cook over a low heat for 5 minutes until the fish is just cooked through. Serve with couscous.

prawn, tomato & fennel tagine

Serves **4**
Preparation time **10 minutes**
Cooking time about
  30 minutes

2 **fennel bulbs,** trimmed and
  thickly sliced lengthways
3 tablespoons **olive oil**
15 g (½ oz) **butter**
2–3 teaspoons **turmeric**
1 **onion,** finely chopped
2 **garlic cloves,** finely chopped
25 g (1 oz) **fresh root ginger,**
  peeled and finely chopped
500 g (1 lb) **raw peeled**
  prawns
1 teaspoon **smoked paprika**
1 teaspoon **sugar**
400 g (13 oz) **can tomatoes,**
  drained of juice
small bunch of **coriander,**
  chopped
bunch of **flat leaf parsley,**
  chopped
salt and **pepper**

Place the fennel in a steamer basket and steam for
5–6 minutes to soften. Refresh under cold running
water, drain and pat dry.

Heat 1 tablespoon of the oil and the butter in a heavy-
based frying pan, add the fennel and cook for 3–4
minutes on each side until golden brown. Toss in
1–2 teaspoons of the turmeric and set aside.

Heat the remaining oil in the base of a tagine or a
large, heavy-based frying pan over a medium heat,
stir in the onion, garlic and ginger and cook for
1–2 minutes until beginning to colour. Add the prawns
and cook for 2–3 minutes until they turn pink, then
stir in the remaining turmeric and the paprika. Add the
sugar, tomatoes and half the herbs. Cover and cook
gently for 10 minutes.

Stir in the fennel, re-cover and cook for a further
5 minutes. Season, garnish with the remaining herbs
and serve with crusty bread or couscous, if liked.

For spicy turmeric & lime prawns, heat
2 tablespoons olive oil in a frying pan or tagine
over a medium heat, stir in 2 chopped garlic cloves,
1–2 deseeded and chopped chillies and 1 tablespoon
chopped preserved lemon rind (see page 18) and cook
for 1–2 minutes to let the flavours mingle. Stir in 450 g
(14½ oz) raw peeled prawns and cook for 2–3 minutes.
Stir in 2 teaspoons turmeric and the juice of 2 limes,
heat and season. Garnish with a chopped bunch of
coriander and serve with warm flatbreads or couscous.

fish with tamarind & potatoes

Serves **4**
Preparation time **10 minutes**,
  plus soaking
Cooking time **30–40 minutes**

100 g (3½ oz) **dried tamarind
  pulp**
300 ml (½ pint) **warm water**
2 tablespoons **olive oil**
1 **onion**, halved and sliced
1–2 **fresh chillies**, deseeded
  and finely sliced
3–4 **garlic cloves**, chopped
1 teaspoon **cumin seeds**
8–10 small **new potatoes**,
  peeled
2 teaspoons **ground turmeric**
1 teaspoon **ground fenugreek**
1 x 400 g (13 oz) **can plum
  tomatoes**
1–2 teaspoons **sugar**
1 kg (2 lb) **fish steaks**, such
  as **sea bream** or **sea bass**
small bunch of **coriander**,
  coarsely chopped
sea salt and **black pepper**

Soak the tamarind pulp in a bowl with the measurement water for 20 minutes. Squeeze the tamarind pulp in your hand to separate the pulp from the seeds and stalks, then strain the pulp through a sieve. Reserve the strained pulpy liquid.

Heat the oil in the base of a tagine or heavy-based saucepan over a medium heat, stir in the onion, chilli, garlic and cumin seeds and cook for 2–3 minutes to let the flavours mingle. Toss in the potatoes and cook for a further 2–3 minutes.

Stir in the powdered spices, tomatoes and sugar and pour in the tamarind water. Bring to the boil, then reduce the heat, cover and cook gently for 15–20 minutes. Season with salt and pepper.

Place the fish steaks in the tagine or saucepan, re-cover and cook the fish gently for 15 minutes. Stir in half the coriander, garnish with the remaining coriander and serve with a salad, if liked.

For prawns with tamarind, soak and strain the tamarind as above. Heat the oil in the base of a tagine or heavy-based saucepan, stir in the onion, garlic and cumin and cook for 2–3 minutes. Toss in 700 g (1½ lb) prawns, washed and deveined, and cook for 2–3 minutes, then pour in the tamarind water. Cover and cook gently for 10 minutes to allow the flavours to mingle. Garnish with the coriander and serve.

fish with leeks, sage & thyme

Serves **4–6**
Preparation time **20 minutes**
Cooking time about
  25 minutes

2–3 tablespoons **olive oil**
1 **onion**, finely chopped
1 **green chilli**, deseeded and
  finely chopped
2–3 **garlic cloves**, finely
  chopped
1 teaspoon **cumin seeds**
2 **leeks**, trimmed and finely
  chopped
a few **thyme sprigs**
small bunch of **sage**, chopped
1 x 400 g (13 oz) **can plum
  tomatoes**, drained of juice
600 ml (1 pint) **fish stock**
4 **fish fillets**, such as **sea
  bass, haddock** or **trout**, cut
  into bite-sized chunks
sea salt and **black pepper**

Heat the oil in the base of a tagine or a large, heavy-based saucepan over a medium heat, stir in the onion, chilli, garlic and cumin seeds and cook for 2–3 minutes to let the flavours mingle. Stir in the leeks and cook for 2 minutes, then add the thyme, sage and plum tomatoes.

Pour in the stock and bring to the boil, then reduce the heat, cover and cook gently for 15 minutes. Season with salt and pepper, then add the fish chunks, re-cover and cook gently for a further 5–6 minutes until the fish is cooked through. Serve with couscous, if liked.

For fish with celery & sage, follow the recipe above, replacing the leeks with 3 trimmed and diced celery stalks and omitting the thyme.

sardines with onions & parsley

Serves **3–4**
Preparation time **10 minutes**
Cooking time **15 minutes**

2–3 **sardines**, about 450 g
  (14½ oz) each, scaled,
  gutted and cleaned
sea salt
bunch of **flat leaf parsley**
2 **onions**, finely sliced
4–5 **peppercorns**
1–2 tablespoons **olive oil**
400 ml (14 fl oz) **fish stock** or
  wine, or a mixture of the two
1 teaspoon **paprika**,
  to sprinkle

Rub the fish with salt inside and out.

Place the parsley leaves in the base of a tagine or heavy-based saucepan, put the fish on top, drizzle with the olive oil and scatter over the onions and peppercorns.

Pour in the stock or wine and bring to the boil, then reduce the heat, cover and cook gently for 15 minutes until the fish is cooked through. Sprinkle the paprika over the fish and serve with chunks of crusty bread to mop up the cooking juices, if liked.

For mussels with onions, preserved lemon & parsley, follow the recipe above, replacing the sardines with approximately 900 g (2 lb) mussels, cleaned and prepared following the instructions on page 132. Discard any mussels that have not opened by the end of the cooking time. Add the finely chopped rind of 1 preserved lemon with the onions and peppercorns and increase the liquid to 600 ml (1 pint).

citrusy prawns with garlic

Serves **3–4**
Preparation time **10 minutes**
Cooking time **5–7 minutes**

2–3 tablespoons **olive oil**
2–3 **garlic cloves**, finely
  chopped
finely chopped rind of 1
  preserved lemon
  (see page 16)
15–16 **fresh king prawns**,
  peeled to the tails and
  deveined
juice of **1 lime**
small bunch of **coriander**,
  finely chopped
sea salt and **black pepper**

Heat the oil in the base of a tagine or a large, heavy-based saucepan over a medium heat, add the garlic and preserved lemon rind and cook for 2–3 minutes to let the flavours mingle.

Add the prawns, stir to coat well and cook for 3–4 minutes until they turn opaque. Stir in the lime juice and coriander and season with salt and pepper. Serve with couscous, if liked.

For prawns with garlic, crushed walnuts & lemon, heat the 2–3 tablespoons olive oil in the base of a tagine or a large, heavy-based saucepan. Stir in 2–3 finely chopped garlic cloves, 150 g (5 oz) crushed walnuts and 15–16 fresh king prawns, peeled to the tails and deveined, and cook for 3–4 minutes until they turn opaque. Add the juice of 1 lemon, season with salt and pepper and serve immediately.

squid & olives with red wine

Serves **4**
Preparation time **25 minutes**
Cooking time **about
45 minutes**

2–3 tablespoons **olive oil**
1 **onion**, finely sliced
3–4 **garlic cloves**, finely
chopped
fresh squid, about 700 g
(1½ lb), cleaned and cut
into thick rings
3–4 tablespoons **black olives**,
pitted
1–2 teaspoons **ground
cinnamon**
2 **bay leaves**
1–2 teaspoons **sugar**
300 ml (½ pint) **red wine**
small bunch of **flat leaf
parsley**, finely chopped
small bunch of **dill**, finely
chopped
sea salt and **black pepper**
1 **lemon**, cut into wedges,
to serve

Heat the oil in the base of a tagine or a large,
heavy-based saucepan over a medium heat, stir
in the onion and garlic and cook for 2–3 minutes
to soften a little. Add the squid, stir to coat well and
cook for 2–3 minutes, then add the olives, cinnamon,
bay leaves and sugar.

Pour in the wine and bring to the boil, then reduce the
heat, cover and cook gently for 35–40 minutes until
most of the liquid has reduced and the squid is tender.
Season with salt and pepper and stir in the herbs. Serve
immediately with lemon wedges and chunks of crusty
bread to mop up the sauce, if liked.

For scallops & olives with red wine, follow the recipe
above, replacing the squid with 500 g (1 lb) cleaned
scallops and replacing the black olives with
2 tablespoons green olives, pitted and cut in half.
Reduce the cooking time to 20 minutes.

fish baked with tomatoes & chillies

Serves **4**

Preparation time **20 minutes**

Cooking time **30 minutes**

3 tablespoons **olive oil**

5–6 **vine tomatoes**, finely sliced

2 **garlic cloves**, finely chopped

2 **green chillies**, deseeded and finely sliced

700 g (1 ½ lb) **firm-fleshed fish fillets**

juice of **1 lemon**

15 g (½ oz) **butter**, cut into small pieces

1 teaspoon **ground cinnamon**

2 teaspoons **sesame seeds**, toasted

sea salt and **black pepper**

Grease the base of a tagine or large overproof dish with 1 tablespoon of the oil.

Arrange most of the tomato slices over the base and sprinkle over half the garlic and chillies. Place the fish in a single layer on top of the tomatoes, scatter over the remaining garlic and chillies and arrange the remaining tomato slices on top of the fish.

Mix the remaining olive oil together with the lemon juice in a small bowl. Pour the mixture over the fish and tomatoes and season. Cover and place in a preheated oven, 180°C (350°F), Gas Mark 4, for 20 minutes.

Scatter the butter over the tomatoes and sprinkle the cinnamon and sesame seeds over the top. Return the tagine to the oven, uncovered, for 10 minutes until the fish is cooked through. Serve with couscous and a salad, if liked.

For fish with baked tomato & cinnamon purée, bake 5–6 tomatoes in an ovenproof dish in a preheated oven, 180°C (350°F), Gas Mark 4, for 15–20 minutes until the skins wrinkle. Remove the skin from the tomatoes, cut into quarters and deseed, then dice the flesh. Put the tomatoes into a food processor or blender and process to a smooth purée. Add 2 teaspoons honey and 1 teaspoon ground cinnamon to the purée and season with salt and pepper. Place 700 g (1 ½ lb) firm-fleshed fish fillets in the base of a tagine and pour over the tomato purée, adding add a little water, if necessary, to cover the fish. Cover and place in a preheated oven, 180°C (350°F), Gas Mark 4, for 20 minutes until the fish is cooked through.

sea bass & aubergine

Serves **4**
Preparation time **15 minutes**
Cooking time **25–30 minutes**

1 **aubergine**, thickly sliced
4 **spring onions**, trimmed and
cut into bite-size pieces
1 **chilli**, deseeded and sliced
25 g (1 oz) **fresh root ginger**,
peeled and grated
700 g (1½ lb) **sea bass**, cut
into chunks
125 ml (4 fl oz) **white wine
vinegar**
125 ml (4 fl oz) **water**
sea salt and **black pepper**
bunch of **flat leaf parsley**,
coarsely chopped, to garnish

Arrange the aubergine slices in the base of a tagine
or a large, heavy-based saucepan and scatter over
the spring onions, chilli and ginger. Place the fish
chunks on top.

Pour over the vinegar and measurement water and
season with salt and pepper. Bring to the boil, then
reduce the heat, cover and cook gently for 25–30
minutes until the fish is cooked through. Garnish with
the parsley and serve with couscous, if liked.

For prawns, spring onions, garlic & vinegar, arrange
500 g (1 lb) shelled, fresh prawns in base of a tagine
or a large, heavy-based saucepan. Scatter over 3 finely
sliced spring onions and 40 g (1½ oz) fresh root ginger,
peeled and finely chopped. Pour over 125 ml (4 fl oz)
vinegar and 125 ml (4 fl oz) water and season with
salt and pepper. Bring to the boil, then reduce the heat,
cover and cook gently for 10 minutes until the flavours
have mingled. Garnish with a bunch of coarsley chopped
flat leaf parsley and serve with couscous.

trout with harissa & puréed dates

Serves **2**
Preparation time **30 minutes**
Cooking time **about
35 minutes**

225 g (7½ oz) **ready-to-eat
soft, pitted dates**
2 tablespoons **argan oil**
1 **onion**, finely chopped
2 **garlic cloves**, crushed
1–2 teaspoons **harissa paste**
1 **trout**, gutted, cleaned
and cut into chunks,
approximately 900 g (2 lb)
bunch of **coriander**, finely
chopped
sea salt and **black pepper**

Put the dates in a food processor or blender with
1–2 tablespoons water and process to form a smooth
purée. (If the dates are not soft they will need to be
soaked in water for several hours first.)

Heat the oil in the base of a tagine or a large, heavy-
based saucepan over a medium heat, stir in the onion
and garlic and cook for 2–3 minutes to soften a little.
Add the harissa and trout chunks and stir to coat well.

Add the date purée and pour in enough water to cover
the fish. Season with salt and pepper. Cover and cook
gently for 30 minutes until the fish is cooked through.
Stir in most of the coriander and garnish with the
remainder. Serve with couscous, if liked.

For trout with dates, follow the recipe above, omitting
the date purée and adding 150 g (5 oz) soft, pitted
dates to the tagine just before the harissa and trout
chunks. Pour over the juice of 1 lemon and enough water
to just cover the fish and continue to cook as above.

chickpeas, beans & lentils

chickpeas & spinach with yogurt

Serves **4**
Preparation time **20 minutes**
Cooking time **12–18 minutes**

1 tablespoon **olive oil**
1 **onion**, finely chopped
2 **garlic cloves**, finely chopped
25 g (1 oz) **fresh root ginger**,
   peeled and finely chopped
1 teaspoon **cumin seeds**
2 x 400 g (13 oz) **cans
   chickpeas**, rinsed and
   drained
1–2 teaspoons **ras el hanout**
500 g (1 lb) **spinach**, steamed
   and roughly chopped
150 ml (¼ pint) **water**
sea salt and **black pepper**
4 tablespoons thick, set
   yogurt, to serve

Heat the olive oil in the base of a tagine or a large, heavy-based saucepan over a medium heat, stir in the onion, garlic, ginger and cumin seeds and cook for 2–3 minutes to let the flavours mingle. Add the chickpeas and stir to coat well, then stir in the ras el hanout and add the spinach.

Pour in the measurement water, bring to the boil, then reduce the heat, cover and cook gently for 10–15 minutes to let the flavours mingle. Season to taste with salt and pepper. Serve as a snack or side dish with dollops of yogurt and chunks of fresh crusty bread, if liked.

For chickpeas & kale with yogurt, replace the spinach with 500 g (1 lb) curly kale, trimmed, steamed and roughly chopped, and follow the recipe above.

butter beans with olives

Serves **4**

Preparation time **15 minutes**, plus soaking

Cooking time **1 hour 25 minutes**

175 g (6 oz) **dried butter beans**, soaked in water for 6 hours or overnight

2 tablespoons **olive oil**

knob of **butter**

2 **garlic cloves**, finely chopped

1 **onion**, finely chopped

1–2 **chillies**, deseeded and finely chopped

1–2 teaspoons **coriander seeds**

1 teaspoon **sugar**

2–3 tablespoons **black olives**, pitted

juice of **1 lemon**

12 **cherry tomatoes**

1–2 teaspoons **dried thyme**

sea salt and **black pepper**

small bunch of **flat leaf parsley**, coarsely chopped, to garnish

Drain and rinse the soaked butter beans. Cook them in a large saucepan of boiling water for 5 minutes, then reduce the heat and simmer gently for about an hour until the beans are tender but not mushy. Drain and refresh them under running cold water.

Heat the olive oil and butter in the base of a tagine or large, heavy-based saucepan over a medium heat, stir in the garlic, onion, chillies, coriander seeds and sugar and cook for 2–3 minutes to let the flavours mingle.

Add the drained butter beans, olives and lemon juice and season with salt and pepper. Cover and cook gently for 10 minutes. Add the tomatoes and thyme, re-cover and cook gently for a further 5–10 minutes. Garnish with the flat leaf parsley and serve with chunks of crusty bread, if liked.

For butter beans with peppers & olives, soak and cook the dried butter beans as above. Add 1–2 red or yellow peppers, cored, deseeded and sliced, to the tagine or saucepan with the garlic, onions, chillies, coriander seeds and sugar and cook for 2–3 minutes. Add the drained butter beans, olives, lemon juice and thyme, cover and cook gently for 15 minutes. Omit the tomatoes. Season the tagine and garnish with the flat leaf parsley.

haricot beans with harissa

Serves **4**

Preparation time **10 minutes**, plus soaking

Cooking time **about 1¼ hours**

225 g (7½ oz) **dried haricot beans**, soaked in water for 6 hours or overnight
2 tablespoons **olive oil**
knob of **butter**
2 **onions**, finely chopped
2 **garlic cloves**, finely chopped
1–2 teaspoons **harissa paste**
2 x 400 g (13 oz) **cans chopped tomatoes**
1–2 teaspoons **sugar**
small bunch of **flat leaf parsley**, finely chopped
small bunch of **fresh coriander**, finely chopped
sea salt and **black pepper**

Drain and rinse the soaked haricot beans. Place them in a large saucepan and cover them with plenty of water. Bring to the boil, then reduce the heat and simmer for about 30 minutes until tender. Drain thoroughly.

Heat the oil and butter in the base of a tagine or a large, heavy-based saucepan over a medium heat, stir in the onions and garlic and cook for 2–3 minutes to soften them a little. Add the drained haricot beans, stir in the harissa, tomatoes and sugar, then cover and cook gently for about 30 minutes.

Stir in half the parsley and coriander, season to taste with salt and pepper and cook gently for a further 5 minutes. Garnish with the remaining parsley and coriander and serve with toasted flat breads, if liked, or as a side dish.

For haricot beans with celery & harissa, follow the recipe above, adding 2 chopped celery sticks to the tagine with the haricot beans, omitting the tomatoes and sugar. Stir in the harissa with half the herbs and pour in enough water to just cover the beans. Bring to the boil, then reduce the heat, cover and cook gently for 25–30 minutes. Season well and garnish with the remaining herbs.

brown lentils with ras el hanout

Serves **4**
Preparation time **5 minutes**
Cooking time **about
   40 minutes**

2 tablespoons **smen**
   (see page 20) or **ghee**
1 **onion**, finely chopped
2 **garlic cloves**, finely chopped
1 teaspoon **sugar**
225 g (7½ oz) **dried brown
   lentils**, rinsed and drained
2 teaspoons **ras el hanout**
600 ml (1 pint) **water**
sea salt and **black pepper**
small bunch of **coriander**,
   finely chopped, to garnish

Heat the smen or ghee in the base of a tagine or a large, heavy-based saucepan over a medium heat, stir in the onion, garlic and sugar and cook for 2–3 minutes to soften a little. Add in the lentils, stir to coat well, then stir in the ras el hanout.

Pour in the measurement water, bring to the boil, then reduce the heat, cover and cook gently for about 35 minutes until the lentils are tender but not mushy. Season well with salt and pepper and garnish with the coriander. Serve as a side dish or as a snack with a dollop of yogurt and toasted flat breads, if liked.

For brown lentils with potatoes, follow the recipe above, adding 4 medium potatoes, peeled and diced, to the sautéed onion and garlic and cooking for 1–2 minutes before adding the lentils and ras el hanout. Increase the measurement water to 750 ml (1¼ pints) and continue to cook as above.

chickpeas & chorizo

Serves **4**
Preparation time **10 minutes**
Cooking time **15–20 minutes**

2–3 tablespoons **argan** or
   olive oil
1 **onion**, halved and sliced
2 **garlic cloves**, chopped
200 g (7 oz) **chorizo**, sliced
2–3 **bay leaves**
several **thyme sprigs**
2 x 400 g (13 oz) **cans**
   chickpeas, rinsed and
   drained
juice of 2 **lemons**
sea salt and **black pepper**
1–2 teaspoons **smoked**
   paprika, to sprinkle

Heat the oil in the base of a tagine or a large, heavy-based saucepan over a medium heat, stir in the onion and garlic and cook for 2–3 minutes to soften a little. Add the chorizo, bay leaves and thyme sprigs and cook for a further 2 minutes, then add the chickpeas.

Pour in the lemon juice, cover and cook gently for 10–15 minutes to let the flavours mingle. Season to taste with salt and pepper. Sprinkle over the paprika and serve with chunks of bread, if liked.

For chickpeas & merguez sausage with sage,
replace the chorizo with 200 g (7 oz) sliced merguez sausage and follow the recipe above, using 1 tablespoon crumbled dried sage leaves instead of the bay leaves and thyme.

spiced green lentils with tomatoes

Serves **4**

Preparation time **5 minutes**

Cooking time **about 35 minutes**

2 tablespoons **argan oil**

2 **onions**, finely chopped

4 **garlic cloves**, finely chopped

2 teaspoons **ground turmeric**

2 teaspoons **ground fenugreek**

225 g (7½ oz) **dried green lentils**, rinsed, picked over and drained

1 x 400 g (13 oz) **can chopped tomatoes**

2 teaspoons **sugar**

750 ml (1¼ pints) **water**

small bunch of **coriander**, finely chopped

sea salt and **black pepper**

Heat the oil in the base of a tagine or a large, heavy-based saucepan over a medium heat, stir in the onions and garlic and cook for 2–3 minutes to soften a little. Add the turmeric, fenugreek and lentils and stir to coat well, then stir in the tomatoes and sugar.

Pour in the measurement water and bring to the boil, then reduce the heat, cover and cook gently for about 30 minutes until the lentils are tender but not mushy, adding a little more water if necessary. Stir in half the coriander and season with salt and pepper. Serve as side dish to grilled or roasted meat and poultry.

For yellow spit peas with tomatoes & ginger,

replace the lentils with 225 g (7½ oz) yellow split peas. Follow the recipe above, adding 40 g (1½ oz) fresh root ginger, peeled and finely chopped, to the tagine or saucepan with the onions and garlic, cook for 2–3 minutes, then stir in the turmeric and split peas and proceed as above.

bean & chickpea k'dra with lamb

Serve **6–8**

Preparation time **25 minutes**, plus soaking

Cooking time **2 hours 40 minutes**

6–8 trimmed **lamb shanks**

3 tablespoons **olive oil**

1 tablespoon **butter**

12 **shallots**, peeled

3–4 **celery sticks**

2 **carrots**, peeled

4–6 **garlic cloves**, chopped

2 teaspoons **cumin seeds**

3 **cinnamon sticks**

175 g (6 oz) **dried chickpeas**, soaked in water for 6 hours and drained

175 g (6oz) **dried kidney** or **fava beans**, soaked in water for 8 hours and drained

2 x 400 g (13 oz) **cans chopped tomatoes**

1.2 litres (2 pints) **lamb** or **chicken stock**

sea salt and **black pepper**

To garnish

large bunch of **mint**, finely chopped

finely chopped rind of 1 **preserved lemon** (see page 16)

Put the lamb shanks in a large saucepan and cover them with water. Bring to the boil and remove any scum from the surface of the water. Reduce the heat and simmer for 1 hour. Remove the shanks and drain.

Heat the oil and butter in a large copper pot or heavy-based saucepan over a medium heat, add the lamb shanks and cook for 3–4 minutes, turning occasionally, until browned all over. Remove the lamb shanks and set aside.

Chop the celery and carrots into bite-sized pieces and add them to the pan with the shallots and garlic and cook for 2–3 minutes, then add the cumin seeds, cinnamon sticks, chickpeas, kidney or fava beans and tomatoes and return the shanks to the pot or saucepan. Pour in the stock and season well with salt and pepper. Bring to the boil, then reduce the heat, cover and cook gently for 1½ hours.

Mix together the chopped mint and preserved lemon in a bowl and sprinkle the mixture over the k'dra. Serve with chunks of bread, if liked.

For bean & chickpea k'dra with beef, replace the lamb shanks with 1.25 kg (2½ lb) lean beef, cut into large chunks and follow the recipe above. Garnish the k'dra with a bunch of finely chopped parsley combined with 1 tablespoon finely chopped preserved lemon rind and 1 deseeded and finely chopped red chilli.

chickpea & chicken k'dra

Serves **6–8**
Preparation time **10 minutes**, plus soaking
Cooking time **about 1 hour 10 minutes**

3 tablespoons **argan** or **olive oil**
knob of **butter**
2 **onions**, finely chopped
6 **garlic cloves**, finely chopped
1 tablespoon **coriander seeds**
8 **chicken thighs**, trimmed
225 g (7½ oz) **dried chickpeas**, soaked in water for 6 hours or overnight and drained
1 tablespoon **ground turmeric**
2 teaspoons **smoked paprika**
900 ml (1¼ pints) **chicken stock**
small bunch of **flat leaf parsley**, coarsely chopped
small bunch of **fresh coriander,** coarsely chopped
sea salt and **black pepper**

Heat the oil and butter in a large copper pot or heavy-based saucepan over a medium heat, stir the onions, garlic and coriander seeds and cook for 2–3 minutes to let the flavours mingle. Add the chicken thighs, stir to coat well and cook for a further 2–3 minutes turning occasionally until lightly brown all over, then toss in the chickpeas, turmeric and paprika.

Pour in the stock and bring to the boil, then reduce the heat, cover and cook gently for about 1 hour until the chicken is very tender. Season to taste with salt and pepper, then stir in most of the parsley and coriander. Garnish with the remaining herbs and serve with flat breads and salad, if liked.

For chickpeas with lamb, turmeric & paprika,
follow the recipe above, replacing the chicken thighs with 8 lamb chops. Finely chop a bunch of mint and add it to the dish at the end of the cooking process with the chopped parsley and coriander.

beans & peppers with harissa

Serves **4–6**
Preparation time **10 minutes**,
  plus soaking
Cooking time **1 hour**
  15 minutes

225 g (7½ oz) **dried butter
  beans**, soaked for 6 hours or
  overnight
225 g (7½ oz) **dried kidney
  beans**, soaked overnight
2 tablespoons **olive oil**
knob of **butter**
2 **onions**, finely chopped
4–6 **garlic cloves**, smashed
2 teaspoons **sugar**
2 teaspoons **cumin seeds**
2 red, orange or yellow
  peppers, cored, deseeded
  and diced
1–2 teaspoons **harissa paste**
2 x 400 g (13 oz) **cans
  chopped tomatoes**
small bunch of **mint**, finely
  chopped
sea salt and **black pepper**

Drain and rinse the butter and kidney beans. Place them in a large saucepan filled with water. Bring to the boil, then reduce the heat and simmer for about 40 minutes until tender. Drain and refresh under cold running water, then remove any loose skins.

Heat the oil and butter in the base of a tagine or a large, heavy-based saucepan over a medium heat, stir in the onions, garlic and sugar and cook for 2–3 minutes to soften. Add the cumin seeds and peppers and cook for a further 1–2 minutes, then add the drained beans and stir to coat well.

Stir in the harissa and the tomatoes and cook over a gentle heat for 30 minutes. Season to taste with salt and pepper, then stir in half the mint and garnish with the remaining mint. Serve with chunks of bread and a dollop of creamy yogurt, if liked, or as an accompaniment to meat and poultry tagines.

For beans with mint & feta, follow the recipe above, omitting the peppers, harissa and tomatoes, and adding in 1-2 teaspoons dried mint and the juice of 1 lemon instead. Cover and cook gently for 10–15 minutes, then stir in the chopped fresh mint, crumble 150 g (5 oz) feta cheese over the top, and serve with toasted flat breads.

baked beans with chorizo & wine

Serves **4**

Preparation time **15 minutes**,
plus soaking

Cooking time about **1 hour**

175 g (6 oz) **dried black-eyed
beans**, soaked in water for
6 hours or overnight

2 tablespoons **smen**
(see page 20) or **ghee**

1 **onion**, coarsely chopped

2–3 **garlic cloves**, finely
chopped

2 **chillies**, deseeded and finely
chopped

1 teaspoon **cumin seeds**

1–2 teaspoons **coriander
seeds**

700 g (1 ½ lb) **small Spanish
chorizo**, sliced

3 **bay leaves**

1 x 400 g (13 oz) **can
chopped tomatoes**, drained
of juice

150 ml (¼ pint) **white wine**

bunch of **fresh flat leaf
parsley**, roughly chopped

sea salt and **black pepper**

Drain and rinse the black-eyed beans. Place them
in a large saucepan filled with water. Bring to the boil,
then reduce the heat, cover and cook gently for about
25 minutes until tender. Drain and refresh the beans
under cold running water and pick out any loose skins.

Melt the smen or ghee in the base of a tagine over a
medium heat, stir in the onion, garlic, chillies and spices
and cook for 2–3 minutes to let the flavours mingle.
Add the chorizo, stir to coat well and cook for a further
2–3 minutes, then add the drained black-eyed beans,
bay leaves and tomatoes.

Pour in the wine, cover and place in a preheated
oven, 180°C (350°F), Gas Mark 4, for 25–30 minutes.
Season to taste with salt and pepper, then stir in most
of the parsley. Garnish with the remaining parsley and
serve with chunks of crusty bread, if liked.

For borlotti beans with peppers and wine, replace
the black-eyed beans with 225 g (7 ½ oz) dried borlotti
beans. Soak the borlotti beans in water for 6 hours,
then rinse and drain. Cook them in a large saucepan
of boiling water for 30 minutes, then drain and refresh
under cold running water. Then follow the recipe above,
also replacing the chorizo with 2 red, yellow or orange
peppers, cored, deseeded and diced

garlicky green lentils with carrots

Serves **4–6**
Preparation time **20 minutes**
Cooking time **about
  25 minutes**

175 g (6 oz) **dried green
  lentils**, rinsed, picked over
  and drained
3–4 tablespoons **olive oil**
1 **onion**, coarsely chopped
6–8 **garlic cloves**, coarsely
  chopped
1 teaspoon **coriander seeds**
handful of **dried sage leaves**
1–2 teaspoons **sugar**
2–3 **carrots**, peeled and sliced
1–2 tablespoons **tomato
  purée**
300 ml (½ pint) **water**
salt and **black pepper**
bunch of **sage**, coarsely
  chopped, to garnish
1 **lemon**, cut into wedges,
  to serve

Bring a saucepan of water to the boil. Add the lentils, reduce the heat and simmer for 10 minutes. Drain and refresh under cold running water.

Heat the oil in the base of a tagine or a large, heavy-based saucepan over a medium heat, stir in the onion, garlic, coriander seeds, dried sage leaves and sugar and cook for 2–3 minutes to let the flavours mingle. Add the carrots and cook for a further 1–2 minutes, then add the drained lentils and stir in the tomato purée.

Pour in the measurement water, bring to the boil, then reduce the heat, cover and cook gently for about 20 minutes until most of the liquid has been absorbed. Season with salt and pepper, garnish with the fresh sage leaves and serve with the lemon wedges to squeeze over.

For garlicky haricot beans with sage, replace the lentils with 225 g (8 oz) haricot beans. Soak the beans in water for 6 hours, then rinse and drain. Place the beans in a large saucepan and cover them with plenty of water. Bring to the boil, then reduce the heat and simmer for about 30 minutes until tender. Drain thoroughly. Follow the recipe above, adding the drained beans to the tagine or saucepan with the onion, garlic, coriander seeds, sugar and dried sage leaves. Omit the carrots and stir in the tomato purée. Pour in enough water to just cover the beans, cover and cook gently for about 15 minutes. Season to taste with salt and pepper, then garnish with the fresh sage leaves. Serve as an accompaniment to meat and poultry tagines.

chickpeas with roasted chestnuts

Serves **4**
Preparation time **20 minutes**
Cooking time **30–35 minutes**

1–2 tablespoons **smen**
(see page 20) or **ghee**
2 **red onions**, halved and
sliced
4 **garlic cloves**, chopped
2 teaspoons **coriander seeds**
1 teaspoon **cumin seeds**,
crushed
1 teaspoon **fennel seeds**
2 x 400 g (13 oz) **cans
chickpeas**, rinsed and
drained
450 g (14½ oz) **roasted
chestnuts**, shelled
1–2 teaspoons **ras el hanout**
1 x 400 g (13 oz) **can
chopped tomatoes**,
drained of juice
1–2 teaspoons **sugar**
small bunch of **flat leaf
parsley**, chopped
sea salt and **black pepper**

Heat the smen or ghee in the base of a tagine or a
large, heavy-based saucepan over a medium heat,
stir in the onions and garlic with the coriander, cumin
and fennel seeds and cook for 2–3 minutes to let the
flavours mingle. Add the chickpeas, stir to coat well
and cook for a further 1 minute, then add the chestnuts
and ras el hanout.

Stir in the tomatoes and sugar and add enough water
to just cover the chickpeas and chestnuts. Bring to
the boil, then reduce the heat, cover and cook gently
for 25–30 minutes. Season to taste with salt and
pepper, then stir in most of the parsley. Garnish with the
remaining parsley and serve with chunks of fresh crusty
bread, if liked.

For butter beans with almonds & ras el hanout,
follow the recipe above, replacing the chickpeas
with 2 x 400 g (13 oz) cans butter beans, rinsed and
drained, and replacing the chestnuts with 225 g
(7½ oz) blanched almonds.

lentils with celery & carrots

Serves **4**
Preparation time **15 minutes**
Cooking time **30–35 minutes**

2 tablespoons **argan** or **olive oil**
1–2 teaspoons **caraway seeds**
4 **garlic cloves**, finely chopped
1 **chilli**, deseeded and finely chopped
2 **carrots**, peeled and diced
2 **celery sticks**, trimmed and diced
175 g (6 oz) **dried brown lentils**, rinsed and drained
600 ml (1 pint) **chicken** or **vegetable stock**
small bunch of **flat leaf parsley**, finely chopped
sea salt and **black pepper**
1 **lemon**, cut into wedges, to serve

Heat the oil in the base of a tagine or a large, heavy-based saucepan over a medium heat, stir in the caraway seeds, garlic and chilli and cook for 1–2 minutes to let the flavours mingle. Add the carrots and celery, stir to coat well and cook for a further 1–2 minutes, then add the lentils.

Pour in the stock and bring to the boil, then reduce the heat, cover and cook gently for 25–30 minutes until the lentils are tender but not mushy. Season to taste with salt and pepper, then stir in the parsley. Serve as a side dish with wedges of lemon to squeeze over it.

For lentils with celery & harissa, heat the oil in the base of a tagine or a large, heavy-based saucepan, stir in 2 finely chopped garlic cloves and cook for 1–2 minutes. Trim and dice 2 celery sticks and add them to the garlic. Stir in 1–2 teaspoons harissa paste, then add 225 g (7½ oz) rinsed and drained brown lentils and pour in 600 ml (1 pint) water. Bring to the boil, reduce the heat, cover and cook gently for 25–30 minutes. Season and serve as above.

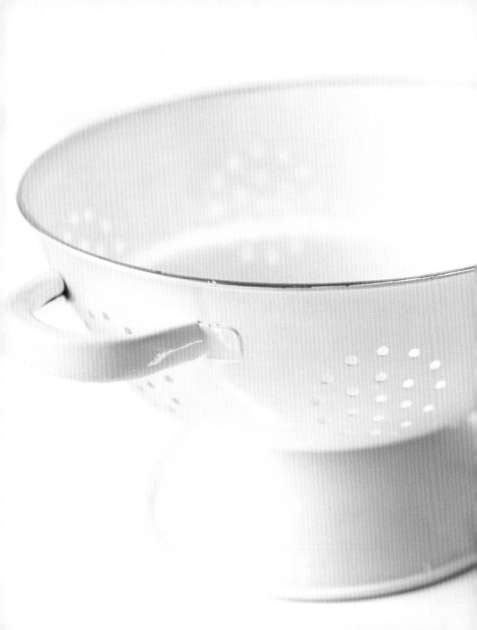

vegetables

runner beans with tomato & dill

Serves **4**
Preparation time **10 minutes**
Cooking time **about**
  45 minutes

2 tablespoons **olive** or **argan**
  oil
1–2 **onions**, roughly chopped
2 **garlic cloves**, roughly
  chopped
500 g (1 lb) **runner beans**,
  trimmed and cut into
  3 or 4 pieces
2 teaspoons **sugar**
juice of 1 **lemon**
2 x 400 g (13 oz) cans
  chopped tomatoes
bunch of **dill,** roughly chopped
sea salt and **black pepper**
small bunch of **flat leaf**
  parsley, finely chopped,
  to garnish

Heat the oil in the base of a tagine or a large, heavy-based saucepan over a medium heat, stir in the onions and garlic and cook for 2–3 minutes until they begin to soften.

Add the runner beans and stir to coat well, then stir in the sugar, lemon juice, tomatoes and dill. Cover and cook gently for about 40 minutes until the beans are tender and the tomato sauce is fairly thick. Season to taste with salt and pepper, then garnish with the parsley. Serve with chunks of fresh crusty bread and bowl of thick, creamy yogurt, if liked.

For green beans with mint, follow the recipe above, replacing the runner beans with 500 g (1 lb) trimmed green beans and replacing the dill with a bunch of roughly chopped mint. Serve with chunks of fresh crusty bread and a bowl of thick, creamy yogurt.

aubergine & courgette tagine

Serves **6**
Preparation time **15 minutes**
Cooking time **about
  45 minutes**

3–4 tablespoons **olive oil**
knob of **butter**
1 **onion**, chopped
2–3 **garlic cloves**, chopped
2 **aubergines**, cut into bite-
  sized chunks
2 **courgettes**, cut into
  bite-sized chunks
175 g (6 oz) **ready-to-eat
  dried apricots**, halved
2 teaspoons **ras el hanout**
2 teaspoons **sugar**
2 x 400 g (13 oz) **cans
  chopped tomatoes**
small bunch of **flat leaf
  parsley**, finely chopped
small bunch of **coriander**,
  finely chopped
sea salt and **black pepper**

Heat the oil and butter in the base of a tagine or a large, heavy-based saucepan over a medium heat, stir in the onion and garlic and cook for 1–2 minutes until they begin to soften. Stir in the aubergines and courgettes and cook for a further 3–4 minutes, then add the apricots, ras el hanout and sugar.

Stir in the tomatoes with half the herbs and bring to the boil, then cover, reduce the heat and cook over a medium heat for 30–40 minutes. Season to taste with salt and pepper, then garnish with the remaining parsley and coriander. Serve with a dollop of creamy yogurt and chunks of fresh, crusty bread if liked.

For aubergines with dates, follow the recipe above, omitting the courgettes, increasing the number of aubergines to 3 and replacing the apricots with 200 g (7 oz) ready-to-eat dried dates, halved lengthways.

eggs with onions, chilli & sage

Serves **4**
Preparation time **5 minutes**
Cooking time **10 minutes**

2 tablespoons **olive oil**
2 **onions**, finely sliced
2 **garlic cloves**, finely chopped
½ teaspoon **sugar**
1 teaspoon **dried chilli flakes**
4–5 **dried sage leaves**,
   crumbled
4 large **eggs**
sea salt and **black pepper**

Heat the oil in the base of a tagine or a large, heavy-based saucepan over a medium heat, stir in the onions, garlic and sugar and cook for 3–4 minutes until they begin to soften and colour. Stir in the chilli flakes and the dried sage leaves and cook for a further 1 minute.

Use a wooden spoon to create 4 wells in the onion mixture and crack the eggs into them. Cover and cook over a medium heat for a further 3–4 minutes until the whites of the eggs are firm. Season with salt and pepper and serve immediately on toasted flat breads or with a dollop of thick yogurt, if liked.

For eggs with black olives and parsley, heat the oil in the base of a tagine or a large, heavy-based saucepan over a medium heat, stir in 2 tablespoons black olives, pitted and finely sliced, and 2 finely chopped garlic cloves, omitting the sugar, and cook for 2–3 minutes. Finely chop a small bunch of parsley and add most of it to the olives and garlic. Crack the eggs over the top, cover and cook for about 4 minutes until the whites of the eggs are firm. Season with salt and pepper and scatter the remaining of the parsley over the top.

spicy roasted cherry tomatoes

Serves **4**

Preparation time **10 minutes**

Cooking time **25–35 minutes**

450 g (14½ oz) **cherry tomatoes**

2 tablespoons **olive oil**

4 **garlic cloves**, halved and smashed

1–2 teaspoons finely chopped **dried red chillies**

1 teaspoon **sugar**

finely chopped rind of
  1 **preserved lemon**
  (see page 16)

sea salt

Put the tomatoes in the base of a tagine or ovenproof dish, drizzle over the oil, scatter the garlic, chillies and sugar over the tomatoes and toss to coat well.

Place, uncovered, in a preheated oven, 200°C (400°F), Gas Mark 6, for 20–25 minutes until the tomato skins begin to wrinkle.

Sprinkle half the preserved lemon rind over the tomatoes and stir to coat well, then season with salt. Return to the oven for 5–10 minutes. Serve with chunks of crusty bread or with grilled and roasted dishes, if liked.

For roasted cherry tomatoes with feta & mint, put 450 g (14½ oz) cherry tomatoes in the base of a tagine or ovenproof dish, drizzle over 2 tablespoons olive oil, scatter over 4 garlic cloves, halved and smashed and 1 teaspoon sugar and toss to coat well. Place, uncovered, in a preheated oven, 200°C (400°F), Gas Mark 6, for 20–25 minutes, then toss in 1–2 teaspoons dried mint and scatter 150 g (5 oz) crumbled feta cheese over the top. Return to the oven for 5–10 minutes. Garnish with 1 tablespoon finely chopped mint.

garlic & ginger sweet potatoes

Serves **4**

Preparation time **15 minutes**

Cooking time **45–50 minutes**

2–3 **sweet potatoes**, peeled
and cut into bite-sized
chunks

3 tablespoons **olive** or **argan
oil**

25 g (1 oz) **fresh root ginger**,
peeled and cut into very thin
sticks

2–3 **garlic cloves**, peeled
and cut into thin sticks

sea salt and **black pepper**

small bunch of **coriander**,
finely chopped, to garnish

Put the sweet potato chunks in the base of a tagine or ovenproof dish, drizzle over the oil and toss in the ginger and garlic.

Place the tagine, uncovered, in a preheated oven, 200°C (400°F), Gas Mark 6, for 45–50 minutes until the sweet potato is tender and some pieces are slightly caramelized. Season to taste with salt and pepper. Garnish with the coriander and serve as a side dish with roasted or grilled meats or with couscous, if liked.

For roasted butternut squash with honey & ginger,

peel, deseed and chop 1 large butternut squash into bite-sized pieces. Put the squash chunks in the base of a tagine or ovenproof dish, drizzle over 2 tablespoons olive oil and toss in 1 tablespoon peeled and finely chopped fresh root ginger. Place the tagine in the oven as above and roast the squash for about 30 minutes until tender. Drizzle over 1 tablespoon runny honey, stir to coat well and return the tagine to the oven for a further 10 minutes. Season to taste with salt and pepper and serve as a side dish to grilled and roasted meats or with couscous.

artichokes with potatoes & peas

Serves **4–6**
Preparation time **10 minutes**
Cooking time **about
25 minutes**

2 tablespoons **olive oil**
1 **onion**, halved and finely
   sliced
2 **garlic cloves**, crushed
1 teaspoon **coriander seeds**
1 teaspoon **cumin seeds**
2 teaspoons **ground turmeric**
1–2 teaspoons **dried mint**
4 small **potatoes**, peeled and
   quartered
300 ml (½ pint) **vegetable**
   or **chicken stock**
3 ready-prepared **artichoke
   bottoms**, quartered
225 g (8 oz) fresh, podded
   peas
finely shredded rind of
   ½ **preserved lemon**
   (see page 16)
sea salt and **black pepper**
small bunch of **coriander**,
   finely chopped, to garnish

Heat the olive oil in the base of a tagine or a large, heavy-based saucepan over a medium heat, stir in the onion and cook for 3–4 minutes until it begins to soften. Add the garlic, coriander and cumin seeds, turmeric and dried mint, then toss in the potatoes, making sure they are coated in the spices.

Pour in the stock and bring to the boil, then reduce the heat, cover and cook gently for 5–6 minutes. Add the artichokes and stir to combine, then re-cover and cook for 10 minutes. Stir in the peas and preserved lemon rind and cook, covered, for a further 5 minutes until the peas are tender. Season to taste with salt and pepper, then scatter the coriander over the top. Serve with chunks of fresh crusty bread or couscous, if liked.

For artichokes with broad beans, place 4 ready-prepared artichoke bottoms hollow-side up in the base of a tagine or a large, heavy-based saucepan. Mix together 2 tablespoons olive oil, the juice of 1 lemon and 2 tablespoons water in a bowl and pour the mixture over the artichokes. Cover and cook over a medium heat for about 15 minutes. Add 225 g (7½ oz) fresh, podded broad beans, sprinkle over 1 teaspoon of sugar and scatter with 1 tablespoon finely chopped dill. Re-cover and cook for 5–6 minutes until the broad beans are tender. Season to taste and serve with couscous.

yam with shallots & prunes

Serves **4**
Preparation time **15 minutes**
Cooking time **about
 40 minutes**

2–3 tablespoons **olive oil**
knob of **butter**
25 g (1 oz) **fresh root ginger**,
 peeled and finely chopped
1–2 **cinnamon sticks**
8 small shallots, peeled
700 g (1½ lb) **yam**, peeled
 and cut into bite-size chunks
175 g (6 oz) **ready-to-eat
 pitted prunes**
1 tablespoon **honey**
400 ml (14 fl oz) **vegetable
 or chicken stock**
small bunch of **coriander**,
 finely chopped
small bunch of **mint**, finely
 chopped
sea salt and **black pepper**

Heat the olive oil and butter in the base of a tagine or a large, heavy-based saucepan over a medium heat, stir in the ginger, cinnamon sticks and shallots, toss to coat well and cook for 2–3 minutes until the shallots begin to colour, then add the yam and cook for a further 2–3 minutes.

Add the prunes and honey and pour in the stock. Bring to the boil, then reduce the heat, cover and cook gently for about 25 minutes. Toss in most of the herbs, season to taste, and cook for a further 5–6 minutes to let the flavours mingle. Garnish with the remaining herbs and serve immediately with plain, buttery couscous, if liked.

For yam with carrots and sultanas, replace the shallots with 2–3 carrots, peeled and cut into bite-size chunks, and substitute the prunes with 150 g (5 oz) sultanas. Follow the recipe above and serve as a side dish with grilled or roasted meats, or with couscous.

butternut squash with sultanas

Serves **4**
Preparation time **15 minutes**
Cooking time **about**
  30 minutes

2 tablespoons **olive oil**
knob of **butter**
8 **shallots**, peeled
4 **garlic cloves**, peeled and
  lightly smashed
125 g (4 oz) **sultanas**
1–2 teaspoons **harissa paste**
1–2 tablespoons **honey**
1 large **butternut squash**,
  peeled, deseeded and cut
  into bite-size chunks
sea salt and **black pepper**
a small bunch **fresh coriander**,
  finely chopped, to garnish
1 **lemon**, cut into quarters,
  to serve

Heat the oil and butter in the base of a tagine or a large, heavy-based saucepan over a medium heat, stir in the shallots and garlic and cook for 2–3 minutes until they begin to soften and colour. Add the sultanas, harissa and honey, then toss in the butternut squash, making sure it is coated in the spicy mixture.

Pour in enough water to cover the base of the tagine or saucepan, bring to the boil, then reduce the heat, cover and cook gently for about 20 minutes until the squash is tender. Season to taste with salt and pepper, scatter the coriander over the top and serve with wedges of lemon to squeeze over it.

For butternut squash with apple, heat 2 tablespoons olive oil and a knob of butter in the base of a tagine or a large, heavy-based saucepan over a medium heat, stir in 1 finely chopped onion and cook for 2–3 minutes until it begins to soften. Stir in 1–2 teaspoons harissa paste, 1 butternut squash, peeled, deseeded and cut into bite-sized chunks, and 2 apples, cored and thickly diced, and proceed with the rest of the recipe as above.

herby baby aubergines

Serves **4**

Preparation time **10 minutes**

Cooking time **about
50 minutes**

2 tablespoons **olive oil**

knob of **butter**

1 **onion**, halved and sliced

3–4 **garlic cloves**, chopped

1–2 **red chillies**, deseeded
and sliced

1–2 teaspoons **coriander
seeds**

1 teaspoon **cumin seeds**

1–2 teaspoons **sugar**

12 **baby aubergines**, left
whole with stalk intact

2 x 400 g (13 oz) **cans
chopped tomatoes**

bunch of **mint**, finely chopped

bunch of **coriander**,
finely chopped

sea salt and **black pepper**

Heat the oil and butter in the base of a tagine or
a large, heavy-based saucepan over a medium heat,
stir in the onion and garlic and cook for 2–3 minutes
until they begin to soften and colour. Stir in the chillies,
coriander and cumin seeds, and sugar and cook for
1–2 minutes, then toss in the baby aubergines,
making sure they are coated in the spices.

Pour over the tomatoes, cover and cook gently for
about 40 minutes until the aubergines are beautifully
tender. Toss in half the mint and coriander, season to
taste with salt and pepper, then re-cover and simmer
for a further 5 minutes. Garnish with the remaining mint
and coriander and serve hot with couscous and yogurt,
if liked.

For baby courgettes with mint, replace the baby
aubergines with 12 baby courgettes. Follow the recipe
above but reduce the cooking time to 30 minutes after
adding the tomatoes and omit the coriander and double
the quantity of mint.

pepper, olive, feta & egg tagine

Serves **4**

Preparation time **10 minutes**

Cooking time **14–18 minutes**

2 tablespoons **olive oil**

1 teaspoon **cumin seeds**

1 teaspoon **coriander seeds**

1 **green, red and yellow
pepper**, all cored, deseeded
and finely sliced

2 tablespoons pitted and
halved **black olives**

150 g (5 oz) **feta cheese**,
cubed

4 **eggs**

pepper

shredded **basil leaves**,
to garnish

Heat the oil in the base of a tagine or a large, heavy-based frying pan over a medium heat, stir in the cumin and coriander seeds and cook for 1–2 minutes to let the flavours mingle. Add the peppers and cook for a further 2–3 minutes, then stir in the olives. Cover, reduce the heat and cook over a medium heat for 5 minutes until the peppers have softened.

Add the feta and cook for 2–3 minutes until it begins to soften, then make 4 wells in the mixture. Break the eggs into the wells, cover and cook for 4–5 minutes until the whites are firm. Grind pepper over the eggs, garnish with the basil leaves and serve with warm crusty bread, if liked.

For spiced tomatoes & eggs with roasted red peppers, heat 1–2 tablespoons ghee in the base of a tagine or a large, heavy-based frying pan over a medium heat, stir in 1 teaspoon each of coriander seeds and cumin seeds and 2 crushed garlic cloves and cook for 1–2 minutes to let the flavours mingle. Top with 3–4 sliced tomatoes, then break over 8 eggs. Cover and cook over a medium heat for 6–8 minutes until the eggs are firm. Season, garnish with roasted red peppers from a jar, sliced, and scatter over a chopped small bunch of flat leaf parsley. Serve on buttered, toasted flatbreads.

lemony okra & tomatoes

Serves **4**

Preparation time **20 minutes**

Cooking time **about 25 minutes**

500 g (1 lb) **okra**, washed and trimmed

juice of 1 **lemon**

2 tablespoons **olive oil**

1 **onion**, halved and finely sliced

2 **garlic cloves**, finely chopped

1–2 **red chillies**, deseeded and finely chopped

2 teaspoons **coriander seeds**

1–2 teaspoons **sugar**

1 x 400 g (13 oz) **can chopped tomatoes**

sea salt and **black pepper**

finely sliced rind of ½ **preserved lemon** (see page 16), to garnish

Place the okra in a non-metallic bowl, pour over the lemon juice and leave to stand for 10–15 minutes.

Heat the oil in the base of a tagine or a large, heavy-based saucepan over a medium heat, stir in the onion, garlic, chillies, coriander seeds and sugar and cook for 2–3 minutes until the onion starts to soften.

Add the okra and lemon juice and stir in the tomatoes, then cover and cook gently for 20 minutes until the okra is cooked through but still retaining its crunch. Season to taste with salt and pepper. Garnish with the preserved lemon and serve with couscous, if liked.

For okra with ginger & preserved lemon, combine 500 g (1 lb) okra with the juice of 1 lemon in a non-metallic bowl and leave to stand for 10–15 minutes. Heat 2 tablespoons olive oil in the base of a tagine or heavy-based saucepan over a medium heat, stir in 2 finely chopped garlic cloves, 1 deseeded and finely chopped chilli and 40 g (1½ oz) fresh root ginger, peeled and finely chopped, and cook for 2–3 minutes to let the flavours mingle. Drain the okra, pat dry with kitchen paper, then add to the garlic, ginger and chillies and toss to coat well. Cover and cook gently for 3–4 minutes until the okra is cooked through but still retains its crunch. Serve with couscous or as an accompaniment to tagines.

sweet potatoes with green olives

Serves **4**
Preparation time **20 minutes**
Cooking time **30–35 minutes**

3–4 tablespoons **olive oil**
  or **argan oil**
1 **onion**, coarsely chopped
25 g (1 oz) **fresh root ginger**,
  peeled and grated
1–2 teaspoons **cumin seeds**
500 g (1 lb) **sweet potatoes**,
  peeled and cut into bite-size
  pieces
juice of 1 **lemon**
12 large **cracked green olives**
2–3 tablespoons **orange**
  blossom water
small bunch of **coriander**,
  finely chopped
sea salt and **black pepper**

Heat the oil in the base of a tagine or a large, heavy-based saucepan over a medium heat, stir in the onion, ginger and cumin seeds and cook for 2–3 minutes until the onion starts to soften. Add the sweet potatoes and stir to coat well.

Pour in the lemon juice, then cover and cook gently for 15 minutes. Add the olives and the orange blossom water, re-cover and cook for a further 10–15 minutes to let the flavours mingle. Season to taste with salt and pepper, then stir in the coriander. Serve with couscous, if liked, or as an accompaniment to a meat or poultry tagine.

For green olives with tomatoes & preserved lemon,

heat 2 tablespoons olive oil in the base of a tagine or heavy-based saucepan over a medium heat, stir in 1 finely chopped onion, 2 finely chopped garlic cloves and 2 teaspoons coriander seeds and cook for 2–3 minutes to let the flavours mingle. Toss in 16 large cracked green olives and add 1 x 400 g (13 oz) can chopped tomatoes and 1–2 teaspoons sugar. Cover and cook gently for 15 minutes. Season to taste with salt and pepper, then stir in a small bunch of finely chopped coriander. Serve as an accompaniment to meat and poultry tagines.

baked carrot & potato tagine

Serves **4**
Preparation time **20 minutes**
Cooking time **about
35 minutes**

2–3 tablespoons **olive or
argan oil**
2 **onions**, thickly sliced
4 **garlic cloves**, finely chopped
25 g (1 oz) **fresh root ginger**,
peeled and finely chopped
1–2 **red chillies**, deseeded
and finely chopped
2 teaspoons **cumin seeds**
1 teaspoon **fennel seeds**
4 large **potatoes**, peeled and
thickly sliced
2 large **carrots**, peeled and
thickly sliced
300 ml (½ pint) **vegetable
or chicken stock**
finely sliced rind of
1 **preserved lemon**
(see page 16)
3–4 **tomatoes**, sliced
15 g (½ oz) **butter**, cut into
small pieces
sea salt and **black pepper**
bunch of **coriander**, finely
chopped, to garnish

Heat the oil in the base of a large tagine or a heavy-based saucepan over a medium heat, stir in the onions and cook for 1–2 minutes until they begin to soften. Add the garlic, ginger, chillies, cumin and fennel seeds and cook for a further 1–2 minutes.

Add the potatoes and carrots and pour in the stock. Bring to the boil, then reduce the heat, cover and cook gently for 15 minutes. If cooked in a saucepan, now transfer to a tagine or oven-proof dish.

Stir in the preserved lemon rind, season with salt and pepper and arrange the tomato slices over the top. Dot the tomatoes with the butter, then place the tagine, uncovered, in a preheated oven, 180°C (350°F), Gas Mark 4, for 15 minutes until the tomatoes are lightly browned. Garnish with the coriander and serve with couscous, if liked, or as an accompaniment to meat and poultry tagines.

For baked potato & tomato tagine, make the tagine as above, omitting the fennel seeds and carrots, adding 150 g (5 oz) crumbled feta cheese with the preserved lemon and increasing the quantity of potatoes to 6.

desserts
& drinks

pistachio & raisin couscous

Serves **4**

Preparation time **20 minutes**

Cooking time **about
10 minutes**

250 g (8 oz) **fine couscous**

2 teaspoons **ground
cinnamon**, plus extra for
dusting

½ teaspoon **ground cloves**

1–2 tablespoons **granulated
sugar**

300 ml (½ pint) **boiling water**

1 tablespoon **sunflower oil**

60 g (2¼ oz) **butter**

120 g (4 oz) **shelled unsalted
pistachio nuts**

2–3 tablespoons **sultanas**
or **raisins**

125 ml (4 fl oz) **milk**

125 ml (4 fl oz) **double cream**

4 tablespoons **runny honey**

Put the couscous into a heatproof bowl and stir in
the cinnamon, cloves and sugar. Pour over the boiling
measurement water, cover with a clean tea towel and
leave to stand for 10–15 minutes. Drizzle the oil over
the couscous and, using your fingers, rub the oil into
the grains until light, airy and any lumps are broken up.

Melt the butter in a heavy-based frying pan over a
medium heat, stir in the pistachios and cook for
2–3 minutes until they emit a nutty aroma. Add the
sultanas or raisins and cook until plump, then tip the
mixture over the couscous. Toss well and spoon the
couscous into 4 serving bowls.

Meanwhile, heat the milk and cream in a small
saucepan. Pour over the couscous and drizzle over the
honey. Serve immediately, with a dusting of cinnamon.

For sweet cinnamon couscous balls, tip 350 g
(11½ oz) couscous into a heatproof bowl and just
cover with boiling water. Cover with clingfilm and leave
to stand for 5 minutes, then fluff up with a fork. Leave
to cool slightly then, using your fingers, rub the grains
to loosen and mould small pieces into balls, squeezing
them together. Roll the balls in 2 tablespoons icing
sugar and dust with 1 teaspoon ground cinnamon.

crystallized rose petals

Serves **4**
Preparation time **10 minutes**

2 **egg whites**
2–3 tablespoons **caster sugar**
2 **sweet-scented, opened
  roses**

Line a baking sheet with greaseproof paper. In a spotlessly clean bowl, whisk the egg whites with a hand-held electric whisk until stiff.

Tip the sugar onto a plate. Carefully pull the rose petals off the flower heads. Brush a rose petal with a little egg white, then dip into the sugar. Shake off any excess and place on the greaseproof paper to dry. Repeat with the remaining rose petals. For best results, leave for 1–2 hours until completely dry. Peel off the paper, then use the crystallized petals to decorate puddings, cakes and milk drinks.

For rose syrup cordial, place 450 g (14½ oz) granulated sugar and 225 ml (7½fl oz) water in a heavy-based saucepan and bring to the boil, stirring continuously until the sugar has dissolved. Add the juice of ½ lemon and simmer for 5 minutes. Stir in 100 ml (3½ fl oz) rosewater and simmer for 4–5 minutes. Leave to cool in the pan, then pass through a sieve into a sterilized bottle or jar. To serve, put a few ice cubes into a glass, add 2–3 tablespoons rose syrup and top up with cold water. (The cordial can also be stored in the refrigerator for 3–4 weeks.)

orange & honey puffs in syrup

Serves **4**
Preparation time **15 minutes**
Cooking time **about**
  20 minutes

3 **eggs**
juice of **1 orange**
grated rind of **2 oranges**,
  plus extra to garnish
50 ml (2 fl oz) **sunflower oil**,
  plus extra for deep-frying
2 tablespoons **runny honey**
350 g (11½ oz) **plain flour**,
  plus extra for dusting
1 teaspoon **baking powder**

Syrup
225 g (7½ oz) **granulated**
  sugar
250 ml (8 fl oz) **water**
juice of **1 lemon**
1–2 tablespoons **orange**
  blossom water

Place the eggs, orange juice, orange rind and oil in a bowl and whisk until frothy, then stir in the honey. Sift in 300 g (10 oz) of the flour and the baking powder and beat to form a thick batter.

Make the syrup. Place the sugar and measurement water in a heavy-based saucepan and bring to the boil, stirring until the sugar has dissolved. Stir in the lemon juice, reduce the heat and simmer for 10 minutes until syrupy. Stir in the orange blossom water and simmer over a low heat.

Beat the remaining flour into the batter until it forms a pliable dough. Tip onto a lightly floured surface and roll out to about 5 mm (¼ inch) thick, pulling out the dough until it stops springing back. Using a 5–7 cm (2–3 inch) cutter, cut out about 16 rounds.

Pour enough oil into a saucepan for deep-frying. Heat the oil to 180–190°C (350–375°F), or until a cube of bread browns in 30 seconds. Deep-fry the dough in batches for 2–3 minutes until puffed up and golden brown. Remove with a slotted spoon and drain on kitchen paper. Using tongs, dip the puffs into the syrup and serve immediately, garnished with grated orange rind.

For ice cream with orange & honey sauce, put 125 ml (4 fl oz) water into a small saucepan and stir in 1 teaspoon cornflour until dissolved. Add the grated rind and juice of 1 orange, 2–3 tablespoons orange blossom water and 2 tablespoons honey, then bring to the boil over a medium heat. Reduce the heat and simmer for 3–4 minutes. Serve with vanilla ice cream.

baked figs with honey & spices

Serves **4**
Preparation time **10 minutes**
Cooking time **22 minutes**

12 **ripe fresh figs**
1 tablespoon **ghee** or **butter**,
   plus extra for greasing
2 teaspoons **cardamom
   seeds**
2 **cinnamon sticks**
grated rind of 1 **lemon**
4–5 tablespoons **honey**
icing sugar, for dusting
**strained yogurt, crème
   fraîche** or **clotted cream**,
   to serve

Cut each fig lengthways into quarters, keeping the base
intact, and place in a lightly greased ovenproof dish.

Melt the ghee or butter in a small saucepan over
medium heat, stir in the cardamom seeds, cinnamon
sticks, lemon rind and honey and cook for 2 minutes
until bubbling. Pour the mixture evenly over the figs.

Bake in a preheated oven, 200°C (400°F), Gas Mark
6, for 20 minutes. Serve dusted with icing sugar
accompanied by yogurt, crème fraîche or clotted cream,
to be dolloped into the middle of each fig.

For creamy figs with cinnamon honey, place 8 ripe
fresh figs on a plate and, using a small, sharp knife, cut
a deep cross into the top of each one, keeping the base
intact. Put a spoonful of clotted cream or strained yogurt
into the hollow and drizzle each one with 1 tablespoon
runny honey. Dust with ground cinnamon and serve.

date & pistachio truffles

Serves **4**
Preparation time **18 minutes**
Cooking time **1–2 minutes**

225 g (7½ oz) **shelled
pistachio nuts**
225 g (7½ oz) **ready-to-eat
pitted dates**, chopped
1 tablespoon **orange blossom
water**
1 teaspoon **ground cinnamon**
1 tablespoon **runny honey**
50 g (2 oz) **desiccated
coconut**

Dry-fry the pistachios in a heavy-based frying pan over a medium heat for 1–2 minutes until they begin to colour and emit a nutty aroma. Put into a food processor with the dates and blend to a thick paste.

Transfer the paste to a bowl and knead in the orange blossom water, cinnamon and honey. Roll about 16 small pieces of the mixture into bite-sized balls.

Sprinkle the coconut onto a plate. Roll the truffles in the coconut until evenly coated. Serve with coffee or tea.

For stuffed almond dates, mix together 150 g (5 oz) ground almonds, 60 g (2¼ oz) caster sugar and 1 tablespoon rosewater in a bowl, then work to a smooth, soft paste, adding more rosewater if needed. Place 200 g (7 oz) ready-to-eat pitted dates on a plate and stuff each one with the almond paste. Press the stuffed dates gently to compress the filling, leaving them slightly open to reveal the paste. Serve with coffee or tea.

saffron pears with lavender

Serves **4**
Preparation time **5 minutes**
Cooking time **25 minutes**

300 ml (½ pint) **water**
juice of 1 **lemon**
3–4 tablespoons **honey**
1 **cinnamon stick**
pinch of **saffron threads**
2–3 **dried lavender heads**,
 plus extra to decorate
4 **firm pears** with the stalks
 intact, peeled

Place the measurement water and lemon juice in a heavy-based saucepan and bring to the boil. Stir in the honey, cinnamon stick, saffron threads and lavender heads, reduce the heat and cook gently for 5 minutes.

Add the pears and bring to the boil, then reduce the heat and cook gently for 20 minutes, turning and basting frequently. Serve hot with the cooking liquid drizzled over, decorated with a few lavender petals.

For saffron, pear & lavender tisane, place 4 tall, heatproof glasses on a tray and pour 1 tablespoon boiling water into each. Scatter 3–4 saffron threads into each glass and leave to steep for 2–3 minutes. Add 1 ready-to-eat dried pear and 1 lavender stem to each glass. Top up with boiling water, drizzle in 1–2 teaspoons runny honey to taste and serve as a digestive drink at the end of a meal, or as a pick-me-up drink at any time of day.

almond & cinnamon filo coil

Serves **4**
Preparation time **10 minutes**
Cooking time **20 minutes**

450 g (14½ oz) **ground almonds**
300 g (10 oz) **granulated sugar**
2 tablespoons **ground cinnamon**, plus extra for dusting
2 tablespoons **orange blossom water**
250 g (8 oz) **filo pastry**
50 g (2 oz) **butter**, melted
1 **egg yolk** mixed with 1 tablespoon water, to glaze
icing sugar, for dusting

Line a baking sheet with greaseproof paper.

Put the ground almonds, sugar, cinnamon and orange blossom water into a food processor and blend to a thick paste. Place the filo sheets under a clean, damp tea towel to prevent them drying out.

Brush the top filo sheet with a little melted butter. Roll lumps of the almond paste into fingers, then place end to end in a line inside one edge of the pastry. Tucking in the ends to enclose the filling, roll up to form a long roll about a thumb's-width thick. Place in the centre of the prepared baking sheet, crease the roll like an accordion, then shape it into a coil. Repeat with the remaining sheets of filo, wrapping them tightly around the first coil.

Brush the egg wash over the coil. Place in a preheated oven, 200°C (400°F), Gas Mark 6, for 20 minutes until lightly golden. Dust with icing sugar and a swirl of cinnamon. Serve warm or at room temperature.

For toasted almond & cinnamon fingers, mix together 175 g (6 oz) ground almonds, 3 tablespoons granulated sugar and 1 tablespoon ground cinnamon in a bowl. Add 1 tablespoon softened butter or ghee and work to a paste. Lightly toast 2–3 slices of brown or white bread, crusts removed and cut into fingers, on one side under a preheated grill. Turn them over, smear with the almond paste and toast for 2 minutes. Serve as a hot snack.

moroccan coffee with cardamom

Serves **4**

Preparation time **2 minutes**

Cooking time **8 minutes**

4 coffee cups of **water**, about
  100 ml (3½ fl oz) each

4 **cardamom pods**

4 teaspoons very finely ground
  Arabica coffee

4 teaspoons **sugar**

Place the measurement water and cardamom pods
in a small saucepan and carefully spoon the coffee
and sugar on top. Gently stir the sugar and coffee into
the surface of the water, making sure you don't touch
the bottom of the pan with the spoon.

Bring to just below boiling point over a medium heat,
gradually drawing in the outer edges of the coffee into
the middle to create a froth. Just as the coffee is about
to bubble, spoon some of the froth into 4 coffee cups
and pour in the coffee. Leave to stand for 1 minute
before drinking to let the coffee grains settle at the
bottom of the cups.

For milky cinnamon coffee, place 2 tablespoons
finely ground coffee, 4 cinnamon sticks and 400 ml
(14 fl oz) water in a saucepan and bring to the boil,
stirring continuously, then turn off the heat and leave
to steep for 10 minutes. Strain the coffee, reserving the
cinnamon sticks. Pour back into the pan and heat gently
to just below boiling point. Put 250 g (8 oz) condensed
milk into a separate pan and heat gently to just below
boiling point. Place the reserved cinnamon sticks into
4 cups, mugs or heatproof glasses. Pour in the coffee to
just over halfway, then pour in the condensed milk. Dust
the tops with ground cinnamon and serve immediately.

mint tea with lemon verbena

Serves **4**

Preparation time **20 minutes**

2 teaspoons **Chinese Gunpowder green tea leaves**

2–3 **sugar lumps**, plus extra to taste

large bunch of **peppermint** and garden **mint leaves** and **stems**

small bunch of **lemon verbena leaves** and **stems**

Place the green tea and sugar lumps in a teapot. Pour over a little boiling water and leave to steep for 5 minutes.

Stuff the mint and lemon verbena leaves into the pot, packing them in as tightly as you can. Add more sugar lumps to taste – the sugar enhances the flavour of the mint – and top up the pot with boiling water.

Place the teapot over a pan of boiling water or over a low heat on the hob, or simply cover with a tea cosy. Leave the tea to brew for 10 minutes.

Place 4 tea glasses on a tray. Pour some of the tea into a glass, then tip it back into the pot. Hold the pot high above the glasses and pour slowly so that bubbles form on top of the tea. Serve immediately.

For quick peppermint tea, trim several stems of peppermint to the size of your tea glasses. Place 1–2 leafy stems into each of 4 glasses with 1–2 sugar cubes or 1–2 teaspoons runny honey to taste. Fill each glass with boiling water, cover with a clean tea towel and leave to steep for 2–3 minutes. Serve hot.

hot spicy tea with chillies

Serves **4**
Preparation time **5 minutes**
Cooking time **about**
   20 minutes

2 **cinnamon sticks**
25 g (1 oz) **fresh root ginger**,
   peeled and finely sliced
6 **cloves**
4 **dried red chillies**
600 ml (1 pint) **water**
2–3 tablespoons **honey**
1 **lemon**, cut into 4 thick slices

Place the spices and the measurement water in a medium saucepan and bring to the boil. Reduce the heat and cook gently for 15 minutes. Stir in the honey and simmer for a further 3–4 minutes.

Strain the tea into 4 heatproof glasses, add 1 of the chillies to each and serve with a slice of lemon to squeeze over.

For quick ginger & chilli tea, place 4 thick slices of peeled fresh root ginger, 4 dried red chillies and 400 ml (14 fl oz) boiling water in a saucepan and simmer for 8–10 minutes. Strain the tea into 4 heatproof glasses, add 1 of the chillies to each and sweeten with honey to taste.

index

238

239

acknowledgements

Executive editor: Eleanor Maxfield
Senior editor: Sybella Stephens
Art direction and design: Penny Stock
Photographer: William Shaw
Home economist: Denise Smart
Stylist: Kim Sullivan
Production controller: Sarah Kramer

Photography copyright © Octopus Publishing Group Limited/William Shaw, except the following: copyright © Octopus Publishing Group/Will Heap 17, 25, 27, 29, 33, 37, 41, 43, 53, 61, 71, 85, 89, 91, 97, 101, 107, 109, 131, 139, 141, 207, 217, 219, 221, 223, 225, 227, 229, 231, 233, 235.